TRIBAL STRUGGLE FOR FREEDOM
SINGHBHUM 1820–1858

About the Author

Sunil Kumar Sen (1914-84) completed his M.A., B.L. from Patna University. Study and research remained the passion of his life though law was his profession. Love for the soil to which he was born inspired him to undertake the rare task of reconstructing the history of the glorious anti-British struggle of the tribals of Singhbhum about which there was no in-depth study when he started his work. Rare for his time he could guess, largely because of his empirical experience and continued interaction with tribal intelligentsia, that historicising tribe required invocation of oral sources and a critical examination of archival as well as relevant printed materials. The songs he could collect enriched his understanding of the tribal situation and helped him write a narrative that may claim to have enriched the historiography of tribal uprising in Jharkhand and India.

Tribal Struggle for Freedom
Singhbhum 1820–1858

Sunil Kumar Sen

CONCEPT PUBLISHING COMPANY, NEW DELHI-110 059

Cataloging in Publication Data—DK
Courtesy: D.K. Agencies (P) Ltd. <docinfo@dkagencies.com>

Sen, Sunil Kumar, 1914-1984.
Tribal struggle for freedom : Singhbhum, 1820-1858 / by Sunil Kumar Sen.
p. cm.
Includes bibliographical references (p.)
Includes index.
ISBN 13: 9788180695124
ISBN 10: 8180695123

1. Ho (Indic people)—India—Singbhum—Politics and government—19th century. 2. Adivasis—India—Singbhum—Politics and government—19th century. 3. Singbhum (India)—Politics and government—19th century. 4. India— History—British occupation, 1765-1947. 5. India—History—Autonomy and independence movements. I. Title.

DDC 954.127 008 9 22

ISBN - 13: 978-81-8069-512-4
ISBN - 10: 81-8089-512-3

First Published 2008

Published and Printed by
Ashok Kumar Mittal
Concept Publishing Company
A/15-16, Commercial Block, Mohan Garden
New Delhi-110059 (INDIA)

Phones : 25351460, 25351794
Fax : 091-11-25357103
Email : publishing@conceptpub.com

This humble effort at preserving the memories of the glorious struggle of the inhabitants of Singhbhum for the freedom of the motherland is dedicated to my revered preceptor, Professor Dr. K.K. Datta, M.A., P.R.S., Ph.D., at whose behest I have endeavoured to write this brief history of Singhbhum during the period 1820-1858.

A Tribute to My Father

My father Sunil Kumar Sen (1914-84) completed his M.A, B.L. from Patna University. Having read History under the illustrious tutelage of Dr. S.C. Sarkar, Prof. Y.J. Taraporewala, Dr. K.K. Datta, Prof. S.H. Askari, Dr. J.N. Sarkar and Dr. B.B. Majumdar, study and research remained the passion of his life though law was his profession. He was one among those who helped open a night college named the Tutorial College, which later developed into Tata College, Chaibasa and taught History and Bengali there free of any remuneration after his arduous legal practice at the District Bar, Chaibasa. He began perhaps the singular quest among his contemporaries into the past of the soil to which he was born and for which he felt great pride. Here a coincidence seemed to have helped his mission when the contact with the scions of the illustrious Porahat family in connection with a court case whetted his latent urge for research. Rare for his time he could guess, largely because of his empirical experience and continued interaction with tribal intelligentsia, that historicising tribe required invocation of oral sources and a critical examination of archival and other relevant printed materials. The songs he could collect enriched his understanding of the tribal situation and helped him write a narrative that evinced a rare empathy for the people.

My father remained a living inspiration for all those who studied the tribe. For some he made his text available as a guide. This always did not augur well for him, as some chose to be more than inspired by his facts and approaches by unscrupulously lifting the chapter titles from his writing. He was not aware of the tricks an academic may play, nor he had the necessary link to get his work published when the whole nation was celebrating the centenary of the Great Revolt.

Meanwhile time elapsed to necessitate minor revision and updating which he initiated himself but could not complete. So it devolved on me to do the remaining work more particularly arranging the notes and references in the standard format besides adding the conclusion to significate the songs and integrate them to the scheme of his writing.

This publication joins Jharkhand and the entire nation in celebrating the 175th anniversary of the Kol Rebellion of 1831-32 and the 150th year of the Great Revolt of 1857-58 which the Ho Ulgulan under Arjun Singh constituted a distinguished event.

Shri Ashok Kumar Mittal deserves our heartfelt thanks for fulfilling a long cherished family dream of presenting this monograph to the lovers of the tribe and tribal history.

Asoka Kumar Sen

Chaibasa
24 July 2006

Preface and Acknowledgements

Not for the observance of the common convention of writing a preface as an inseparable part of a book but for bringing home to the mind of the reader the necessity of this book, a necessity having its origin in the inner urge of my mind to discharge the obligation as a student of history and also as one who being born and brought up in the district of Singhbhum must contribute his humble share in building up, on the basis of the evidence that is available as also of tradition, the history of the inhabitants of this part, do I venture to write these few lines as a prologue.

The district of Singhbhum as it is at present carved out by the British rulers for administrative advantages and subsequently extended after the Boundary Commission of 1955 was, in the beginning of the 19th century, known as the south-western frontier of the then 'Lower Provinces' of Bengal. In those days Singhbhum comprised of Kolhan, Porahat and the territories of Seraikella, Kharsawan, Anandpur and Kera. The four southern *pirs*, namely Thai, Lalgarh, Aula and Bharbharia, were the bones of contention between the different local chiefs as also the British East India Company. The Hos, amongst the earliest inhabitants of this land, always believed that all these areas, irrespective of the pretensions of the contending parties, who claimed one portion or the other to be theirs, could ill-afford to part with even an inch of their sacred land. This is the genesis of all the political upheavals of those times in this area.

The period between 1820 and 1858 was in a sense the worst, at the same time, in another sense the best in the history of the Hos; the worst because it ended in a great disaster for them, namely the loss of their independence which they had enjoyed since their advent in Singhbhum and the best because it was during this period that the glorious elements in the character of the Adibasis came to light. It was this period that presented to the world their characteristics and the salient features of their mental make up, that is, solidarity, earnestness, the zeal and fervour to maintain their liberty and, to crown all, their grim determination to do or die.

A student of history must base his arguments on facts, available from the records of contemporary chroniclers whose statements, however, are to be sifted before they are finally incorporated to take the shape of authentic history. Besides documentary evidence tradition has also to be taken into account. I have, in this humble endeavour, tried to collect both although the local inhabitants have only a few traditions on which much reliance can be placed for, as very often one comes across incredible stories which tend to vitiate the real trend of event. It will, however, be unjust to say that there are no memories of the brilliant achievements of their brave ancestors for, indeed, even now the village grandfathers do indulge in narrating across the fire in winter evenings, the stories of the battles fought by the Adibasis for driving out the *Sahibs* and earlier against the Rajas of Chotanagpur and Porahat. The battles fought have been commemorated through songs also which are sung even today in the sylvan solitudes not only of Singhbhum but also of the adjoining Munda-land.

The Ho-land is an integral part of the Sovereign Democratic Republic of India and the glorious history of this part will, I am sure, be a source of inspiration to everyone, not to speak of the children of the soil alone. Since the achievement of freedom there has been a sense of complacency which leads the young Adibasis to forget their past which may infuse in them fresh zeal to keep pace with the march of civilization and induce them to throw off the present tendency of thinking that there is nothing in their history or custom which deserves to be preserved as noble heritage. If the qualities of their ancestors were brought home to their minds as traits of character worth developing, the qualities of sincerity of purpose and proper zeal and fervour for the maintenance of integrity, they may prove themselves worthy citizens of India.

In the collection of the data I have received substantial help from two of my learned friends, namely Sri S.N. Pandey, Advocate, and Sri Sidiu Hembrom, members of the Chaibasa Bar. The former was kind enough to furnish me with records without which it would have been impossible for me to give a correct picture of Singhbhum during 1857-58 and the latter lent me invaluable records which helped me in coming to definite conclusions regarding the activities in the district during 1820-37. I deem it my duty gratefully to acknowledge their debt.

I must make a grateful reference to Sri Rameshwar Prasad Singh Deo, a descendant of the illustrious Porahat family, whose contribution in the shape of supplying me with most valuable documents deserves special mention.

I owe a deep sense of gratitude particularly to Sri Kamakhya Charan Banerji, the then Deputy Inspector of Schools, Chaibasa, whose unfailing enthusiasm and whole-hearted co-operation enabled me to present this humble work. He had been a steady source of inspiration and encouragement to me and laboured with me sincerely and cheerfully.

To the members of Ho Cultural and Literary Society, under the auspices of which the history of the times was read before a distinguished gathering, consisting mainly of the members of the tribe and organized by the Tata College, Chaibasa in the Pillai Town Hall on 16 August 1957 I owe sincere gratitude for their kind appreciation and cordial encouragement.

Lastly, the interest and encouragement of Sri Chandra Mohan Deogam, Deputy Superintendent of Education, deserve grateful acknowledgement especially for the pains taken by him in collecting the beautiful patriotic songs which are still sung in Kolhan.

Shri-Panchami **Sunil Kumar Sen**
(24 January 1958)

Contents

1

The Lion Land and the Arrival of the Singh Dynasty

Hunter has described Singhbhum as 'Sinha-bhoomi', *i.e.* Lion Land.[1] It has vast undulating tract surrounded by long lines of hills swelling to noble heights to the west and southwest of the land. The hilly tract, however, gradually slopes down due to the erosion of the soil and the valleys carved out by rivers like south Koel, which has its meandering course to the south-west, Baitarani, flowing southward and the combined valleys, of Sanjay and Kharkai, tributaries of Subarnarekha, delivering its waves south eastwards and ending in the semi-plateau lands of the district of Midnapur.

The dense and impassable forests of Saranda, affording protection and isolation to the sparse population, have been inaccessible and are so even now at many places. Life in the dense forest region abounding in wild animals was never very secure and the few inhabitants had to be vigilant in the midst of their struggle for existence which has always been very hard. The density gradually diminishes and results in a jungle land where also life is not very easy. No wonder therefore the inhabitants of these barren tracts should be brave and tenacious, not having much to lose whenever a struggle came. No wonder therefore that they should prize their liberty more than their lives.

The majority of the population commonly known as the Hos is a branch of the Munda speaking people mostly inhabiting the district of Ranchi and north and northwestern portions of Singhbhum. The cultural affinity of the Hos, borne out by the commonality of their languages, richly supports the tradition that the ancestors of the Hos migrated from the north and northwestern parts of Chotanagpur plateau. It is not known when the Mundas came, may be in the pre-Aryan era when these people were driven out from the plains and took shelter in the jungles and forest lands like Chotanagpur, inaccessible and barren, which did not attract the attention of the races that invaded from time to time.

It is stated in legends and texts in the *Rig Veda* and the *Bhagavata Purana* that Cherus and Kols occupied the Magadha country at the time of the birth of Gautama Buddha. The sculptures at Bodh Gaya portray not Aryan but Turanian and Kol features. The dominant race Cherus, probably accepted the doctrines of Buddha and became Aryanised, while the Kols rejected them and adhered to the life of freedom. The Kols appear as the earliest settlers in the Gangetic valley. They had been long established there and had attained some advance in civilization, when they were dislodged and driven back by the Savars, a Dravidian people, about 500AD.[2]

The Cheru chiefs, on being expelled from it, fell back into what later constituted the Palamau subdivision of Lohardaga, whilst the chief seat of the Munda race is now the plateau of Chotanagpur proper. The central tableland, on which the tribes rallied, was admirably adapted for defence. The approaches to it from the north, northwest, east and south, were exceedingly precipitous. The paths winding could be defended by a handful of resolute men against hosts of invaders. The highlands in the western and southwestern direction stretched into Sarguja and Jaspur uniting with the Vindhyan mountains in a western direction and the Satpura range to the southwest. They divided the waters of the Narmada and Mahanadi, forming a covered way by which fresh accessions of cognates strengthened the growing colonies of Kols on Jharkhand and forest tracts. Thus were founded the 'strongholds of the ten chiefs', referred to in the *Puranas,* and in Colonial Wilford's essays, as *Dasarna* or ten forts east of the river Sone. These Jharkhand or Chotanagpur chiefs appear to have maintained their isolated and defensive positions throughout the long series of Hindu dynasties, and to have come with an indifferent reputation under the Mohammedan rulers.[3]

Around the 10th century AD the Hos began to migrate from Chotanagpur plateau due to the extension of Hindu power there. They came in sufficient numbers to be able in course of time to defeat the Saraks, Gonds as well as Bhuiyans and conquer a sizeable portion of Singhbhum.[4] After that the Hos successfully maintained their independence for centuries. This was mainly due to the inaccessibility of the area. The barrenness of the land could hardly attract invaders. The Hos appear to have been left alone by the Mohammedans particularly on two grounds, namely the want of desired revenue from these unproductive parts consisting mainly of forest and shrub lands, which earned for the land the name 'Jharkhand' and the difficulty of maintaining administrative control from the far-off Delhi. The earliest Muslim inroads (circa 1616 AD) were directed against Kokrah or Chutia Nagpur proper, which was then known at the Delhi court for the diamonds found in its rivers.[5]

The north of the district came under the rule of the Singh family of Porahat. Tradition ascribes that the family belonged to a branch of the Rathors from Marwar. The emigration of this dismembered branch of the Rathors dates back to the 9th century AD when, it is said, their ancestors, on their way back from Puri, were instrumental in subjugating the Bhuiyans in favour of the Hos who were then at war with them. Ultimately the Rathors obtained sovereignty over both the tribes.[6] This theory of the subjugation of the *Larka* (fighting) Hos by the Rathor family according to Hunter is open to suspicion as 'indirectly supporting their invalid claims to supremacy over the Kols'.[7] The suspicion is untenable because as a matter of fact the *Larka* Hos had thrown off all appearance of subordination to the Raja and other chieftains of Singhbhum and enjoyed perfect independence since circa 1770 AD.[8] It is evident therefore that what might have been the appearance, the subordination was there, and that too from an undated past.

There is yet another theory according to which Akbar's general Man Singh invaded the tracts to support the Bhuiyans against the Hos and subjugated the land and brought it within the Mughal empire. It is further said that that the ancestors of the Porahat family were in the service of the general who entrusted the administration of the newly acquired territory in their hands.[9] This contention does not hold good since it does not appeal to reason that such petty parochial feuds in the remotest and most inaccessible part of the country, unattractive and barren, could assume such dimensions as to receive the attention of the Great Mughal. This is further borne out by the unequivocal statement of Vansittart, then Resident at Midnapur, in his letter of December 1767, addressed to Verelst, Governor of Bengal wherein he says 'Singhbhum was never reduced under the domain of the Mughals but has for 52 generations been an independent district in the possession of the present family.'[10] By 'the present family' Vansittart evidently meant the Porahat family. Taking a generation to comprise 12 years in the minimum, 52 generations would mean as long a period (52 × 12) as 624 years. If we consider that Porahat family had established itself as the ruling family of Singhbhum 624 years before the writing of this letter it means that they were in Singhbhum at least since the middle of the 12th century. It would then be a gross anachronism to think that they had come with Raja Man Singh in the 16th century AD.

The fact, therefore, remains that the Porahat family had settled in the district long before the establishment of Mughal rule in India. The name of the district had its origin in the commemoration of the name of the clan (Singh) to which the founder belonged.[11] According to tradition the first Raja was Kasinath Singh and his capital was at Porahat. However, the more intelligent and educated members of the Ho community, on the other hand, hold that the land was named after *Sing-Bonga* meaning thereby the Sun God.[12] The controversy regarding the name of the district is not one of vital importance in the present context.

The early history of the Singh dynasty is one of the establishment of a consolidated kingdom. It had its capital at

Porahat with the presiding deity Pauri Devi, the benign goddess under whose grace the ruling family was believed to have prospered. Later on Anandpur, Seraikella, and Kharsawan and last of all Kera were carved out from the present state as fiefs or subordinate grants. Seraikella was given to Raja Bikram Singh, the younger son of the family, sometime about the second decade of the 17th century (1620 AD).

From its very inception and right up to 1818 AD Porahat was a sovereign state inasmuch as it was independent both of the Marathas and British who were then busy aspiring for suzerainty in India. This fact finds support from the letter of Vansittart to Verelst, referred to above. For further support we can cull the letter of 17 March 1766 by Vansittart to J. Graham. The former writes 'the jurisdiction of the Marathas had never extended to Singhbhum nor did they receive the smallest revenue from it. But the Marathas maintained some sort of a cordial relation with the ruler of Singhbhum since the Marathas used to attack Orissa through this route.'

These facts clearly indicate that Singhbhum had attracted the attention of the East India Company Government since the 1760s, more so after their control over adjoining Midnapur bestowed to them by Mir Kasim the Nawab of Bengal in 1760. In January 1768 Vansittart was instructed to collect information regarding Singhbhum, particularly to ascertain whether the Marathas had any claim or had ever any pretensions to this area. The Company government could learn that the jurisdiction of the Marathas had never extended to Singhbhum nor did they receive any revenue from Singhbhum.[13] This information proved very vital. In 1773 discovering that the Raja of Singhbhum encouraged smuggling of salt through his territory, which caused economic loss to the Company, Captain Forbes, in course of his expedition to Dhalbhum, forced the Raja to come to his camp and 'execute an obligation never to harbour either ryots or merchants in future.' This was followed by the imposition of similar engagements in 1793 on the rulers of Seraikella and Kharsawan regarding the harbouring of fugitive rebels from British territories.[14] A relation was thus established between the Company government and the chieftains of Singhbhum. This link the English sought to utilize in near future. In his letter written in early September 1803, the Governor General Wellesley requested the ruler of Seraikella 'to take measures to prevent the gang of robbers and the band of adversaries from passing into the country of the English Company', through his territory. Similarly in a letter dated 22 September 1803, Earnest, Magistrate, implored the chief of Seraikella to take 'suitable steps that the Marathas may not pass through the boundaries of your territory and stop supplies to them.'[15]

This was the relation between the English East India Company and the ruler of Seraikella in 1803. The first contact with the Raja of Singhbhum, however, was delayed till 1820, may be with some design to alienate the chief of Seraikella from the rest of the chiefs of Singhbhum. By the time when the Company approached the ruler of Seraikella for assistance there was no obstacle except the Marathas in their ambitious programme of assuming the supremacy in India. Even then they could not but pursue the policy of divide and rule in the case of comparatively insignificant adversaries in Singhbhum by taking advantage of their parochial feuds. And when finally the turn of the Raja of Singhbhum came, it was not a difficult task, since their main adversary the Marathas had been fully subdued by 1818. This victory all the more waxed the strategic significance of Singhbhum because the control over this territory was necessary for connecting their Bengal empire with Cuttack and Sambalpur, the English gains from the third Anglo-Maratha War (1817-18).[16] Accordingly E. Roughsedge, the Political Agent to the Governor General, instructed his assistant Lt. Ruddel in March 1819 to proceed to Porahat to negotiate a settlement with the Raja of Singhbhum and also to collect all possible information regarding the area and the extraordinary race called the *Larkas*.[17] The Raja was also in need of the intervention of the British in fulfilling three-fold selfish ends: to be recognized as lord paramount over the chiefs of Seraikella and Kharsawan, to recover from the ruler of Seraikella the family idol of Pauri Devi and lastly, to obtain British help in reducing the Hos whom he claimed as his subjects.[18] By not recognizing the claim of paramountcy the design of the British in crippling the integrity of the district was achieved. Now they took up the question of utilizing the differences of these chiefs to their advantage.

The British succeeded in forcing Raja Ghanashyam Singh of Porahat in entering into a covenant on 1 February 1820. The *Kabuliyat* reads thus:

> 'Whereas His Excellency the most noble the Governor-General-in-Council has been graciously pleased to extend to me the protection of the Honourable Company, and to admit me within the list of Feudal Tributaries of the British Empire in India, I hereby engage and bind myself and my posterity to a loyal devotion to the interest of my new Sovereign, and the most implicit obedience to such orders as I or they may, from time to time, receive from a competent authority. I further engage for the purpose of marking my Feudal dependence on the British Government to pay an annual tribute of 101 Sicca Rupees to be given with the year 1226 (Ist Bhadon) 1818, and to be paid in the month of Poss, to the person who may be appointed to receive it by His Lordship in Council. Should I or my posterity wilfully fail in the observance of these stipulations, I hereby declare myself and them liable to such notice of, or punishment for, the infringement, as it may appear to the British Government for the time being to deserve.'[19]

A *Patta* was given to the Raja Ghanashyam Singh Deo in acceptance of the *Kabuliyat* on the Ist February 1820 which stated:

> 'In return for the Engagement which you have executed and delivered to Captain Ruddell, I am authorized and directed by the British Government to assure you of the protection of the Honourable Company, the efficient benefit of which, in your maintenance in all your existing rights, privileges, and possessions, you and your posterity will continue to enjoy, so long as you and they shall faithfully abide by the stipulations to which you have pledged yourself and them.'[20]

The Company had also 'intended that similar agreements should be entered into with the Chiefs of Seraikella and Kharsawan.' It was further stated that 'the matter was overlooked at the time.'[21] This shows that there was no such agreement between the English Company and either of the rulers of Seraikella and Kharsawan who probably sidetracked the issue, taking advantage of the eagerness of the Company to enter into a covenant with the Raja of Singhbhum. The Company too, probably, did not foresee in either of these chiefs as formidable an opponent as the Raja of Singhbhum. This proved to be true at a future date when the brave descendant of this dynasty, Raja Arjun Singh, flouted British authority and successfully maintained his independence for a period of eighteen months.

NOTES AND REFERENCES

1. W.W. Hunter, *The Imperial Gazetteer of India*, Vol. XII, London, 1887, p. 529.
2. F. Buchanan, *Journal of Patna and Gaya in 1811-1812*, Superintendent, Government Printing, Bihar and Orissa, Patna, 1925, pp. 36, 123-24, 157.
3. E.T. Dalton, *Descriptive Ethnology of Bengal*, Calcutta, 1872, pp.163-64.
4. Lt. S.R. Tickell, 'Memoir on the Ho desum' (improperly called Kolehan)', *Journal of Asiatic Society of Bengal*, Vol. XI, part II, 1840, pp. 696-97; A.D. Tuckey, *Final Report on the Resettlement of the Kolhan Government Estate in the District of Singhbhum 1913-1918*, Superintendent, Government Printing, Bihar and Orissa, Patna, 1920, pp. 17-8; F.B. Bradley Birt, *Chota Nagpore A Little Known Province of the Empire*, London, 1903, p. 84.
5. E.T. Dalton, *Tribal History of Eastern India, (Original Title Descriptive Ethnology of Bengal)*, Cosmo Publications, Delhi 1973, p. 163fn.
6. Dalton, *Tribal History*, p. 179.
7. T.S. McPherson, *Final Report on the operations for the preparation of a record of rights in Pargana Porahat, district of Singhbhum 1905-7*, Calcutta, 1906, p. 18.
8. Letter of Major E. Roughsedge to C.T. Metcalfe, Secretary to the Government, 9 May 1820, para 9. South-West Frontier Political Despatch Register (SWFPDR), Vol. 27, Bihar State Archives (BSA).

9. L.S.S. O'Malley, *Bengal District Gazetteers: Singhbhum, Saraikela and Kharsawan*, Calcutta, The Bengal Secretariat Depot, 1910, p. 26.
10. *Ibid.*, pp. 1-2.
11. *Ibid.*, p. 31.
12. Other theory to be proposed is that Singhbhum was named after *Singdar* trees with which it was filled. Appendix, Song III.
13. O'Malley, *Bengal District Gazetteer*, pp. 31-32.
14. *Ibid.*, p. 32.
15. N.N. Singhdeo, *Singhbhum, Seraikella and Kharsawan Through the Ages*, Calcutta, no date, pp. 54-56.
16. Roughsedge to John Adam, 12 August 1818, SWFPDR from 12 August 1817 to 15 December 1818, Vol. 25, (BSA).
17. Dalton, *Tribal History*, pp. 180-181.
18. Roughsedge to Metcalfe, 9 May 1820, para 9.
19. C.U. Aitchison, *A Collection of Treatises, Engagements and Sanads relating to India and Neighbouring Countries*, Vol. II, Government of India, Central Publication Branch, Calcutta, 1930, p. 182
20. *Ibid.*
21. W.W. Hunter, *A Statistical Account of Bengal*, Vol. XVII, London, 1877, p. 137.

2

The Alien Enters Singhbhum and the Recoil of the Adibasi

While the Raja of Porahat bartered his freedom with the protection to be given by the British, the indomitable Hos, locally dreaded as the *Larka* Kols, of Kolhan could never think of owing allegiance to any power whatsoever. They could not forget the glorious battles which they had fought and won against their adversaries who dared rob them of their freedom. One was made by Dreepnath Sahi, the grandfather of the present Raja of Chota Nagpur, at the head of more than twenty thousand men being assisted by the Raja of Singhbhum. The *Larkas* drove the enemies away from Singhbhum with heavy losses. Next was by Raja Jagannath Singh of Porahat with almost an equal force about 50 years ago. But his troops were also driven back with heavy casualties. In the beginning of the present century the *Larkas* of a *pargana* in Mayurbhanj were attacked by the zamindar of Bamanghaty of the same district. This attempt also proved abortive and the zamindar lost many of his men. While these successes made the *Larkas* confident of their military strength, these had taken from the Raja of Singhbhum and all the neighbouring chieftains all inclination to molest the *Larkas* on their own ground.[1]

Nor was the Company Government unaware of the valour and tenacity of these *Larkas*. This had prompted the British to seek their assistance in checking the apprehended inroad of the Marathas through the shortest route to Orissa, *i.e.* Kolhan, the land of the *Larkas*. This is borne out by a letter written by one Morgan to Fenwick on the 7 December 1803.[2]

However, any tangible proof of a direct contact between the Hos and the British officials before 1819 is not available. It may be presumed from the comments of British officials quoted below that the latter was mortally afraid, like others, of the Hos who in their turn suspected the foreigners and disliked them. Col. Dalton writes—'The Hos would allow no strangers to settle in or even pass through the Kolhan, and pilgrims to Jagannath had to make a circuit of several day's journey to avoid it.'[3] Major Roughsedge, the Assistant Political Agent, had earlier observed: 'Not having any of the feelings of veneration for Bramins, cows which pervade Hindoos of every description they make no scruple of putting to death any man of respectable caste who presumed to enter their territory, nor is there I can venture to affirm a single Bramin, Rajpoot or Mussulman in anyone of the numerous and well inhabited villages they possess.'[4]

The Company Government directed Roughsedge to proceed to Porahat to negotiate a settlement with the Raja of Singhbhum. He, however, could not penetrate into the heart of the Ho land because of the great fear entertained by him of the nature of the country and the people. The British could not summon courage to initiate an attack all by them. Not only this, Roughsedge spurned Raja Ghanashyam Singh's requests for military assistance in subduing the *Larkas*. Instead he merely attributed the suffering of the people to the attacks by tribesmen and desired that roads be made safe for the passage of British troops.[5] But in an earlier letter dated 3 February 1820 to the government he had expressed his intention to assist the Raja in re-establishing some portion of his influence over the *Larka* Hos which the Raja claimed, his ancestors had possessed.[6]

The causes for the impending tribal resistance against forces which plotted their subjugation were not mere outbursts of emotions arising out of a feeling of being fettered but are to be traceable to other deep-rooted factors. These were the fear of economic subjugation and social humiliation, being similar in nature to those that triggered the later revolt of their Munda brethren of Chotanagpur in 1831-32.[7] The genesis of such recoil of the tribesmen against the intruders has invariably been external domination, their suppression, and flinging of indignity. Neglected alike by society and government, plunged into economic distress and surrounded on all sides by alien fortune seekers they had been forced to a state of desperation which could lead them to one and one path alone that is the desperate struggle for the preservation of their independence. Mr. Cuthbert, Collector of the district of Ramgarh, observed: 'The jagirdars (with few exceptions) have always been considered a turbulent description of people ....The half-deserted villages, which one frequently meets with evince the oppressive conduct of these people as land-holders.'[8]

To the primitive man nothing is dearer than soil and the homestead, carved out by them from the midst of dense forests as preserved in their folklore.[9] It is a possession which he can hardly separate from his very existence. They were naturally apprehensive of the Raja, accompanied by a retinue of *sardars* and soldiery, falling upon the land reclaimed by them with the sweat of their brows nay, with their life-blood and hallowed with memories of their ancestors. This was too much for them to bear. They noticed with alarm that secret negotiations were going on between Raja and the Sahibs to aggravate their piteous plight and to rob them of their freedom for ever. Meanwhile the Mundas in the district of Ranchi goaded to rebellion by the 'oppressive conduct' of the land holders had flared up and this provided additional impetus to their downtrodden compatriots in the district of Singhbhum. Queerly enough, the Rajas of these two regions also stood shoulder to shoulder to quell their unfortunate subjects whose only crime was a desperate bid for freedom, and this is significant of the spirit of the two rival camps. Nor was the third party inactive during all this period. The British were not mere silent spectators to all these events and, like expert opportunists that they were, watched and waited for the time to strike to rob the freedom not only of the Hos but of all those who might stand in their way of fulfilling their dream of the establishment of an Indian empire.

Major Roughsedge, therefore, sympathized with the 'Raja's pretensions' and planned to compel the Hos to submit to the Raja. He was not, however, very confident of his allies, the chiefs of the district, who virtually 'trembled at their own temerity and drew back.' Roughsedge observed, 'They have so formidable an opinion of the power and ferocity of these savages, that, notwithstanding the considerable force under my command, they were evidently much alarmed, and have made a formal protest against the danger of the march.'[10] The 'timid suggestion' was, however, ignored and the march on to Kolhan could not be postponed at any cost though Roughsedge himself was nonetheless shaky.

Instead of immediately risking a direct combat with the Hos Roughsedge intended first to create a cleavage amongst the members of the tribe and then to conquer them piecemeal. Immediately after his arrival at Seraikella on 20 February 1820, he proceeded to win over the Hos of Ajodhya, one of the villages in Kolhan belonging to the Raja, a place about 8 or 10 miles northwest of Chaibasa on the road from Chakradharpur to Seraikella. This he did in concert with Raja Ghanashyam Singh of Singhbhum and his relations. Through the efforts of some influential men Roughsedge could after great difficulty conciliate two Mundas of considerable influence to come to the camps at Seraikella. On being threatened of a military march through the hearts of *Larka* territories and also promised of kind treatment in the event of compliance, these village heads agreed to 'relinquish their predatory habits and pretensions' and 'return under the ancient and legitimate authority of the Rajah of Singhbhum.' They also informed Roughsedge that mainly due to the threats of the 'Kols' of southern *pirs* they had thrown off their obedience to the Raja and they would willingly return to his tutelage if they were provided with necessary protection from the militants.[11]

On the request of the Raja of Singhbhum Roughsedge then encamped at Ajodhyagarh on 18 March for the purpose of conciliating the refractory elements in the vicinity. During his three-day stay twelve Mundas of Ajodhya *pir* came to the camp and made separate agreements with him for the payment of *malguzari*. They were presented with turbans and clothes. They then took leave in good humour. Roughsedge next moved to the head village of Rajabassa *pir* of the same name. He received ambivalent reception there. While some *Larkas* cut through a large embankment draining off water accumulated there, majority of the Mundas of the *pargana* visited Roughsedge. The Major then made usual presents to them in obvious bid to win them over and encouraged them to desist from insurgency. On 25 March he reached Chaibasa in Gumla *pir* and encamped there.[12] Accompanied with a battalion of artillery, cavalry and infantry, the onward march of the British force was carried on with a sense of self-complacency since the Hos offered practically no resistance till then. This was perhaps due to the strategy of the Hos to allow the enemies some ground in the beginning and then to encircle them from all sides. Being confident of the prowess of the British army Roughsedge felt that the enemy would be numbered. The rude surprise however came when he found after entering Chaibasa, the finest among their villages, that the armed enemy had attacked some of his camp followers. He could sense that the enemy had strategically allowed him to enter the heart of Kolhan so that they could be encircled. It has been rightly stated—'apparently the Hos had made up their minds to employ against him the tactics which had been so successful in their encounters with the levies of Chotanagpur.'[13] This statement was obviously referring to the victories of the Hos in their encounter with the confederated army of the Raja of Chotanagpur and the Raja of Singhbhum.

The attack by a band of men, who desperately fought against the superior forces of the British, men so determined and desperate as to ignore volleys of cannon of the British artillery and to rush with battle-axes against an overwhelmingly large army, was indeed an alarming experience even for the mighty British. So Roughsedge thought it wise to guard against fresh attacks. Lieutenant Maitland was, therefore, ordered to proceed with the pickets and a troop of cavalry to pursue and attack offenders and "to cut off the retreat" of the Hos who, after sustaining heavy loss of men, were escaping to the hills evidently to prepare for fresh and more formidable attacks. The pursuit by Maitland was retaliated with heavy showers of arrows. But having found that the arrows could not produce the desired effect the Hos 'with a degree of rashness and hardihood scarcely credible, met the charge of the troop half-way in an open plain, battle-axe in hand.'[14]

Maitland was convinced that slaughter here and there would not be enough to quell these people who could fight undauntedly regardless of any consequence. He did not, therefore, think it prudent to pursue those who had escaped to the hills. Instead he decided to move rapidly towards the village where the grass-cutter had been killed. There he found, standing near the corpse and prepared for action a second party of 60 men who behaved with still greater desperation, rushing at the troop and striking like furies at both horses and men, until the whole were sabred. They directed their attack chiefly at the horses which wounded several of them, while only two *sawars* were wounded.[15]

On his pursuit Maitland was confident that he would not have to face his enemy on the way. In order to strike terror in the minds of inhabitants he killed an innocent grass-cutter. This induced the Hos to retaliation which resulted in the loss which British army had to incur on return journey. That evening Roughsedge found his rear threatened and mails intercepted. The interception of mails meant the loss of contact with headquarters wherefrom he could receive no instructions, and supplies of ration, ammunition or reinforcement.

To add to his embarrassments, Roughsedge received the news that the Hos had assembled in arms at Gutialore. He found that instead of being cowed down taking recourse to force and acts of cruelty, such as the killing of the innocent grass-cutter, had roused the Hos to further action and stronger retaliation. Even then he decided to send a strong party out next day to attack the enemy at Gutialore under Maitland. The Hos were also prepared to meet the enemy. So Maitland was confronted with repeated discharges of arrows, which caused him considerable loss. To drive them from the shelter afforded by the enclosures, he set fire to the village. But still there was an obstinate resistance, resulting in the slaughter of several Hos which ultimately forced them to lay down their arms.[16]

The Hos had however no written language of their own nor was there any person among them who could keep a record of these glorious incidents of bravery and martyrdom. So we have to accept the British version of laying down arms and acceptance of quarter. The indomitable spirit of the Hos, however, found expression in many more incidents similar to that of Gutialore where with equal bravery they fell down before the superior forces of the invader. Glory nevertheless is due to the battleaxe and bow and arrow with which the Hos bravely fought the firearms and cavalry of the enemy. The record of events would have been different could the Hos of the northern and southern *pirs* organize themselves as a whole and offered a joint opposition. The privilege of entrance up to Ajodhya was utilized to the full by the shrewd British Major who could win over and gain valuable information and help from some weaker elements. A greater unity among the Ho would have made the task of the British more difficult. The result was that the Mundas of twenty-four villages of Gumla *pir* tendered their submission to the Raja. It seems unlikely that the whole of northern *pirs* submitted on this occasion.[17] The rather vague information of the submission of the heads of all the *Larka* villages[18] had in fact been the insurgents' ploy to avoid further devastation.[19]

The Lull before the Storm

After his stay in Gumla *pir* for two or three days Major Roughsedge reached the village of Jagannathpur on his way to Sambalpur. The village was within the Satbantari *pargana*. This *pir*, formerly a *khass* possession of the Raja of Singhbhum, had in all sixty villages. The inhabitants of these villages had stopped paying any revenue or showing any allegiance to the Raja. But they were on the whole less hostile to him as compared to their brethren of other parts of Kolhan. They were believed to be willing to submit to the Raja and stop predatory activities but for the fear of reprisals from the more militant men of Jaintgarh in the neighbourhood. With the intention of conciliating these refractory elements Roughsedge reached

Jaintgarh on 1 April 1820. But his overtures met with a rude rebuff. The valiant men of Barndia and Gamaria villages succeeded in mobilizing twelve adjoining villages to stage a formidable resistance to the alien intruders. In this they were joined by the Hos of Thai *pir* who had meanwhile managed to liberate themselves from the throe of Mayurbhanj Raj. But before the enemies could fire the first salvo, on 6 April 1820 the Hos became definitely aggressive and dealt the first blow on the British contingent. Roughsedge ordered his men to take recourse to violent measures. The natural consequence of this was more obstinate resistance. With the timely assistance of the inhabitants of Thai *pir* Ho insurgents had great confidence of overpowering the enemy. Roughsedge found himself in a precarious position as meanwhile he had been cut off from headquarters and deprived of all supplies. Encircled on all sides the Major had no prospect of reinforcement.[20] Thanks to the timely help from Babu Ajambar Singh, son of the ruler of Seraikella, he could escape though not with considerable loss. To this timely rescue he had made grateful reference in his letter addressed to Kuar Bikram Singh, the ruler of Seraikella: 'That your son Babu Ajambar Singh with his runners and sawars served me faithfully, and at the time of punishment and chastisement of the *Larka* people the men with aforesaid Babu showed courage and loyalty in risking their life for us.'[21]

Roughsedge could continue for only ten more days. The only plea that he could find out for retirement from the scene was depletion of provisions and sickness in his camp. Before leaving Jaintgarh, however, he posted one Narayan Singh with 100 *barkandazes* for the protection of Raghunath Bisee, *killedar* of Jaintgarh. But as soon as Roughsedge had left a sizeable number of *Larkas* from Barndia attacked Jaintgarh and finally drove Narayan Singh away. He fled to Porahat, while Raghunath escaped to Keonjhar. The *Larkas* set fire to Jaintgarh village and destroyed it. But soon hostilities broke out between conciliatory and refractory Hos.[22]

Driven away from the southern *pirs*, unsuccessful in creating a division between the Hos of the north and the south and baffled in his last attempt in establishing a post through the help of the 'Hindustani Irregulars', Roughsedge was constrained to seek help from his government. This cry for succour finds expression in the following words:

> 'I am of opinion that the voluntary submission of the Lurkas to the Raja's authority in the degree that it has taken place should be sanctioned and countenanced although without any guarantee of its continuance.'[23]

The government, however, did not think that the actions of the Major were in conformity with their achievements in other parts. They felt that Roughsedge had failed both in respect of military operations and diplomatic relations with the *Larkas*. Even at this stage he could hardly convince the government that there would be any guarantee of the continuance of the little that he professed to have achieved. This prompted the Company government to dispatch a communiqué in July 1820 to the effect that he was not to undertake any operation, political or military, without any express sanction nor was sanction accorded to the measures suggested by him.

The refusal on the part of the government to extend their approval of his actions as well as the future programme chalked out by him was nothing short of a reprimand. But Roughsedge tried to justify his presence in Singhbhum by sending dispatches to the effect that everything was quiet at the southwestern front. Perhaps his action was justified by a report, received from Bahuran Singh, the *subedar* of *barkandazes*, to the effect that the Hos had agreed to pay revenue to the Raja.[24] This might have also lulled Roughsedge to believe that the Hos had finally abandoned the path of belligerence. He informed the government accordingly in his dispatch of 14 November 1820.[25]

The basis of *subedar* Bahuran Singh's report was not wholly untrue. He might have discerned reluctance on the part of the Hos to continue the fight. This he seemed to have interpreted as their inclination to come to terms. On the other hand the apparent inactivity of the Hos was most likely due to their unwillingness to keep aloof from their natural avocations particularly during the harvesting season, as cultivation was the mainstay of their very existence. Roughsedge was misled by the lack of vision and foresight of the *subedar.* He could not visualize that the lull in fact presaged the coming storm. The inevitable retaliation came when the Ho had filled his granary.

NOTES AND REFERENCES

1. Letter of Roughsedge to Metcalfe, Secretary to the Government, dated 9 May 1820, paras 16-17, (SWFPDR, Vol. 27, BSA).
2. The similar request is made in a letter from H. Ernest, Magistrate, to Raja Abhiram Singh dated 22 September 1803, quoted in N.N. Singh Deo, *Singhbhum, Seraikella and Kharsawan—Through the Ages,* Calcutta, No date, pp. 55-56.
3. E.T. Dalton, *Tribal History of Eastern India,* (Original Title *Descriptive Ethnology of Bengal*), Cosmo Publications, Delhi, 1973, p. 179.
4. Roughsedge to Metcalfe, 9 May 1820, para 15.
5. *Ibid.,* paras 10-11, 22.
6. *Ibid.,* para 22.
7. For details see J.C. Jha, *The Tribal Revolt of Chotanagpur (1831-32),* K.P. Jayaswal Research Institute, Patna, 1987.
8. S.C. Roy, *The Mundas and their Country,* Calcutta, 1912, p. 198.
9. See Appendix.
10. L.S.S. O'Malley, *Bengal District Gazetteers: Singhbhum, Saraikela and Kharsawan,* Calcutta, The Bengal Secretariat Depot, 1910, p. 33.
11. Roughsedge to Metcalfe, 9 May 1820, paras 23-24.
12. Letter of Roughsedge to Lt. Col. Nicol dated 31 March 1820, paras 2-3 (SWFPDR, Vol. 26, BSA); Roughsedge to Metcalfe, 9 May 1820, paras 25-26.
13. O'Malley, *Bengal District Gazetteers,* p. 33.
14. Roughsedge to Nicol, 31 March 1820, para 4.
15. *Ibid.,* paras 3-5.
16. *Ibid.,* paras 7-8; O'Malley, *Bengal District Gazetteers,* p. 34.
17. Roughsedge to Metcalfe, 9 May 1820, para 29, O'Malley, *Bengal District Gazetteers,* p. 34.
18. Roughsedge to Nicol, 31 March 1820, para 10.
19. Roughsedge to Metcalfe, 9 May 1820, para 27; Dalton, *Tribal History,* p. 181.
20. Roughsedge to Metcalfe, 9 May 1820, paras 29-31.
21. Letter of Roughsedge to Bikram Singh dated 13 April 1820 (SWFPDR, Vol. 27, BSA).

22. Roughsedge to Metcalfe, 9 May 1820, para 31.
23. Letter of Roughsedge to Metcalfe, dated 19 June 1820 (SWFPDR, Vol. 27, BSA).
24. Report of Bahuran Singh, Subedar of Barkandazes, dated 2 Kartik (October-November 1820) to Major Roughsedge (SWFPDR, Vol. 27, BSA).
25. Letter of E. Roughsedge to G. Swinton, Secretary to the Government dated 17 February 1821, para 5 (SWFPDR, Vol. 27, BSA).

3

The First Struggle for Freedom

The storm appeared with tremendous intensity and vehemence directed against those who sought to subdue the Hos. The British have called this as the 'Kol Rebellion' of 1821. It was the outcome of a genuine desire of the people for maintaining their sylvan solidarity and isolation from outside elements. It was a struggle for independent existence which took the form of an all-out effort to exterminate every trace of alien intrusion. The Hos were determined to do or die.

Only a few weeks after Roughsedge had sent his dispatch of 14 November 1820, a dispatch full of a sense of complacence, alarming reports poured in from all quarters that everything was not well in the south-western front.[1] The Hos of the northern *pirs* had buried all their differences with those in the south for fighting the common enemy and rose in arms. The people of Gumla *pir* took the lead. This *pir* was formerly the possession of the ancestors of Ghasi Singh, its present landlord. The Raja of Singhbhum laid a claim over half of the revenue collected, as the elder branch of the ancestor of Ghasi Singh had no male heir. Ghasi Singh received an occasional rent from the Hos. But spurred by the British victory over the *Larkas* he demanded an inflated amount as rent from them. At this point due to financial crisis Raja Ghanashyam Singh also demanded a sum of two thousand rupees from Ghasi Singh. Accordingly, he ordered Bahuran Singh *subedar* of *barkandazes* stationed in Kolhan to realize the amount. Ghasi Singh proceeded to Gumla *pir* along with Bahuran Singh to effect the collection from the people. But as they declined to pay, Ghasi Singh was compelled to adopt evasive and dilatory steps. Out of anger Bahuran

Singh detained him and extracted a promise that he would clear the dues in fifteen days.[2] This harsh treatment to Ghasi Singh might have instigated the Hos.[3] But there were more plausible grounds. Eighty *barkandazes* who accompanied their *subedar* to Gumla *pir* forcibly took away goat and fowls from the villagers. The pleadings of Ghasi Singh to the *subedar* failed to produce the desired result. Moreover, the troops allegedly misbehaved with the daughter of Khandu Pater, a respectable tribal of the locality.[4]

On 13 Magh corresponding to 31 January 1821 fifteen hundred inhabitants of Gumla *pir*, joined by their kinsmen from Barndia, launched an attack on *subedar*'s troops at Pokhuria, a place two to three miles away from Chaibasa. Though Bahuran Singh was able to repulse this attack, near village Cheri he was confronted with a ferocious band of *Larkas*, armed with axes and swords. The defeat could not be averted. With his fourteen men and twenty horses the *subedar* was killed. Only four injured horsemen could reach Seraikella to inform Bikram Singh about the reverse.[5] After this success the insurgents closed all roads and *ghats*. On 6 February they attacked Raja's garrison in the mud fort of Chainpur which was under the charge of Jamadar Rattan Singh. A party of sixty *barkandazes* from Seraikella reinforced this garrison. But in the encounter they lost twelve men, three horses and all cash, arms and ammunitions.[6]

As the situation had almost gone beyond control, on 17 February 1821 Major Roughsedge applied to government for instructions to counter this emergency.[7] On 21 February the Major received a message from Raja Ghanashyam Singh to the effect that the rebels had devastated his *parganas* of Kula, Chakradharpur, Chainpur and Senai. This alarmed the people to such a degree that they fled away to Anandpur and the Raja himself was also compelled to seek refuge there.[8] On the very next day equally alarming news reached Roughsedge from Chaitan Singh, the chief of Kharsawan, that he was driven to the verge of despair and was in dire need of help.[9] Roughsedge could not comply with the request of either of the chiefs. Probably his previous experience had made him wiser. He, therefore, thought it prudent to gain time and not to precipitate action. In the meantime the Hos of the princely states contiguous to Singhbhum had also been inspired by the noble actions and achievements of their brethren of Singhbhum. Roughsedge wrote to government on 6 March 1821 that the Hos threatened the fifteen outposts on Jackson's Road from Bamanghaty to Bonai with concentrated attack. He requested the government for two companies and half a troop of horse to escort the Raja, who had taken shelter at Anandpur, back to Porahat and to ensure safety and protection to his men.[10]

To cope with the tense situation the British government deemed it necessary to launch a campaign in Kolhan. Accordingly, the Adjutant-General was consulted to formulate a scheme for military operations against the *Larkas*. The Adjutant-General informed Roughsedge that the British offensive was to be led by Lt. Col. Richards. The rulers of Mayurbhanj, Keonjhar and Bonai, through whose states the troops were to pass, were instructed on 17 March to answer Lt. Col. Richards' requisitions and afford every facility for the progress of the troops. The ruler of Mayurbhanj and the zamindar of Ghatsila were also asked to send agents to Midnapur to be in readiness to move with the troops and afford every possible assistance. The Raja of Bonai was asked, besides helping the troops to pass, to be ready to furnish men for intelligence work as might be required by Richards.[11]

Meanwhile the Adibasis were restless and could have no peace until they had expelled the British from their territories. On 21 March 1821, the Thakur of Kera sent information to Roughsedge that a large assemblage of Hos assisted by Ghasi Ray and other *jagirdars* of Tamar had actually attacked Kera on 18 or 19 March 1821. From the acting Magistrate of Ramgarh came a report on 23 March that large bodies of *Larkas* had mobilised on the northern borders of Singhbhum to attack the foreigners. The roads to Tamar and Patkum, where the *Larkas* intended to concentrate, passed through the territory of the Thakur of Kera, who was so helpless that he could not offer even the semblance of an opposition and so had no other alternative but to seek the help of Roughsedge. How far Roughsedge could protect this dependent Thakur was not mentioned in the chronicles of the British officers stationed in Singhbhum in those days. But the very lack of mention suggests that he had not afforded any protection to this helplessly devoted ally who probably was left to his own fate. It is quite likely that the Hos had abandoned the idea of making fresh attacks on Kera or it may be that they had decided to postpone their proposed march northward. The fact, however, remains that the Major and all other British officials had maintained scrupulous silence regarding incidents between 23 March and 8/9 April 1821 by which time Lt. Col. Richards was scheduled to reach Bamanghaty to start British operations. Lord Hastings's government, which had by this time realized that the affairs of Singhbhum were of no mean magnitude and deserved careful consideration and well-planned military operation, could not tolerate the continuance of this state of things over a wide area. The plan formulated by the Adjutant-General therefore intended to encircle the Hos from all sides.

As already stated the government had intimated the rulers of Mayurbhanj, to the south-east of Singhbhum, Keonjhar and Bonai, to the south and south-west respectively, and zamindar of Ghatsila, on the eastern border, to facilitate the progress of the troops under Lt.Col. Richards to whose exclusive direction all military operations were to be conducted. As regards the attack from the north and north-west Froebisher of the Ramgarh corps was to proceed with 400 firelocks, two six-pounders, 100 irregular horsemen to Gumla *pir* via Anandpur and Porahat to deal with the Hos.[12] Froebisher was to be assisted by Captain Raban who was to reach Seraikella from Bankura. The main attack, however, was intended against the southern *pirs* the most intensive centre of Ho belligerence. Lt. Col. Richards was to start his operations from 30 or 31 March 1821, initiating from Midnapur and continuing the March through Bamanghaty to south Kolhan. Evidently, Richards was to enter Kolhan by following a route from Midnapur *via* Chakulia off Haludpukhur towards Bahalda and thence to Katbari and Tantnagar, thus passing through the territories of the zamindars of Midnapur and Ghatshila and the ruler of Mayurbhanj, all of whom were allies of the British. From

Tantnagar he was to proceed through Bharbharia and Bhagabila hill-pass towards Khairpal. The troop under Captain McLeod, which had started from Cuttack and reached Jaintgarh through the western parts of Mayurbhanj, was to meet him at Bantaria through Gamaria (Hat-Gamaria) and Khairpal with the plan of attacking the Hos in their retreats.[13] On 15 April 1821 Richards was joined by Ajambar Singh, the heir-apparent of Seraikella, who had obviously reached there from Seraikella *via* Icha and Rajnagar after crossing the river Kharkai somewhere near about Mirudi. On 16 April 1821 when Richards reached Tantnagar the headman of that place informed him that he was to encounter tough resistance in his planned southward march. Richards first divided his men into three divisions after reaching a *nala* between Tantnagar and Kheriatangar. He then ordered arson on Tantnagar and surrounding villages and captured a large number of helpless men and women from there. The men were imprisoned and the women were compelled to go and inform the headman that he was to surrender within a fixed time.[14] This obviously shows that the headman was not in the village and was evidently with the fighting elements.

The next move of Richards was to send a detachment of a battalion under Captain Savage to capture Bharbharia and to send a regiment to ensure the safety of supplies in his march to Ipilsingi. By this time Richards was convinced that the intended march through Bharbharia and the hill-pass of Bhagabila was fraught with such danger as it would not be safe to undertake the operation. He, therefore, sent a mission across the hills to inform McLeod of his inability to join him according to previous plan on the plea that the hill-pass was not suitable for the passage of artillery. This mission too, it is so alleged in his report, did not succeed in reaching McLeod for want of proper guide. Moreover, Lieutenant Col. Todd, who was sent by Richards to encumber a band of Hos, was not only repulsed but also compelled to beat a retreat with severe losses. A rescuing picket of 40 men also had to come back in the face of stiff opposition. All these constrained Richards to change his whole plan and recall Captain Savage from his way to

Bharbharia. Joined by Captain Savage he marched westward to Chaibasa where he met Captain Raban on 21 April 1821. The dream of encircling the Hos of the south however remained unfulfilled. He changed his direction further and proceeded towards Rajabasa wherefrom he intended to assist Forebisher in the latter's attack on Khuntpani. Captain Raban with his detachment was ordered to join Major Roughsedge at Ajodhya. On 24 April 1821 he joined Roughsedge at Rajabasa. The untold miseries caused by the concentration of troops who mercilessly butchered the Adibasi population, set fire to their villages and went to the extent of imprisoning women so unnerved the Hos that for fear of total annihilation and the loss of honour of their women most of the inhabitants of Gumla *pir* left their hearth and home and sought refuge in the wilds of Saranda. The British issued threats to the Ho headmen asking them to appear personally in camp by the evening of 3 May 1821. Out of panic the tribal heads considered it wise to tender their submission.[15]

At this stage Roughsedge did not think it wise to continue the inhuman operations lest the Hos should be driven to desperation. Instead he wrote to Chief Secretary Swinton to the effect that the policy of suppression and active victimisation might be substituted by one of maintenance of troops at strategic posts to maintain the tranquillity of northern and central *pirs* only. The southern *pirs* were left to themselves but with a threatening post near about Kat-Karanjia within ten miles from Jaintgarh. Perhaps the Hos of the southern *pirs* took recourse to a cessation of hostilities fearing that any overt act on their part might lead to complete annihilation of their brethren of the central and northern *pirs* which had been completely subjected to a reign of terror.[16]

The military operations were, however, to be supplemented with diplomatic missions though not unmixed with threats of rapine and pillage of which there is mention in Roughsedge's letter to Swinton: 'Col. Richards and myself had determined to allow the inhabitants of Goomla (meaning Gumla *pir*) 4 days for the present for personal appearance and submission to the British Government of each head of a village failing that those Sirdars who did not within the time prescribed avail themselves of the terms offered would be considered to have forfeited all claims to clemency.'[17] Naturally, the Hos were forced under dire constraints to capitulate with the motive of saving themselves from dishonour and complete extermination.

The Infamous Agreement of 1821

The victorious aliens forced the agreement of 7 May 1821 on the vanquished Hos. The terms were:

1. "We acknowledge ourselves to be subject to the British Government and engage to be loyal and obedient to its authority.
2. We agree to pay to our chief or zamindar 8 annas for each plough for the five years next ensuing, and afterwards one rupee if our circumstances admit it.
3. We engage to keep the road through our parganas open and safe for all descriptions of travellers, and, if robbery takes place, to deliver the thief to justice and account for the property stolen.
4. We will allow persons of all castes to settle in our villages and afford them protection; we will also encourage our children to learn the Oriya or Hindi tongues.
5. If we should be oppressed by our chiefs or zamindars, we will not resort to arms for redress, but complain to officers commanding the troops on our frontier or to some other competent authority."[18]

It is claimed that the Hos prayed at this time to be taken under the direct rule of the British. But their wishes were not complied with. They were instead compelled to enter into agreement to pay tribute to the chiefs.[19] The proclamations already stated were orders to the Hos to surrender on pain of further acts of atrocities. It is difficult to understand how this could encourage the Hos to come to terms or to go to the extent of praying for being brought under the direct rule of the Company.

This agreement brought in its chain untold sufferings and hardships to the entire Adibasi population of Singhbhum who were now subjected to political bondage over and above the economic burden which the payment of revenue at flat rates according to the number of ploughs entailed. It was more irksome for the fact that money was not easily available to them, their entire economy being based mainly on barter.[20] The continuance of such a state of affairs would mean nothing but disaster. The fire of discontent, therefore, did not take much time to flare up. After a year or two of peace, the *Larkas* again became restive. The assistance rendered by them to the Nagpur Kols some years later during the rebellion of 1831-32 was too palpable a challenge to the government to escape serious notice.

For the time being their latent anger manifested in their resuming the old practices of pillage and plunder, committing raids and laying waste neighbouring villages. As no attempt was made to restore order or seriously to check the predatory predilections they were encouraged to extend the circle of their depredations. They ravaged Dhalbhum, devastated Bamanghaty and penetrated far into Chotanagpur.[21] Though some violence was committed by the Hos in their efforts to emancipate themselves from alien domination this battle to preserve their freedom had been painted in the darkest colours by the British. The poor Hos had no written language of their own to mention their just claims or to register their protests against the inroads of these foreigners whose very presence in their sacred soil was nothing short of a trespass and unjust and uncalled for interference with the affairs of those who had done them no harm and whose only crime lay in their attempt at maintaining their liberty.

Added to the political subjection and economic injuries insults were piled upon the Hos. The institution of Manki and Munda in the tribal society was embodiment of a trust bestowed on these leaders of the community, the Munda for the village and the Manki for the group of villages forming a *pir*.[22] The Hos knew of no other social order. The aliens assailed this sacred institution by compelling them to accept non-Hos as their headman in supercession of the hereditary claims of

Singrai Manki. They felt definitely dishonoured due to the insult flung upon their neighbours of the district of Ranchi which they apprehended might be repeated in their case also in accordance with the third clause of the agreement of 7 May 1821. The Hos rightly apprehended that one intruder thus thrust upon them would bring in his chain many more fortune-seekers and the result would only be the alienation of their land and the contamination of their social order. Such incidents had already occurred in the district of Ranchi in *pargana* Sonepur of Ranchi district contiguous to Bandgaon in Singhbhum. The immediate cause of the revolt in Sonepur was the grants made by the Maharaja's brother of a number of villages there over the heads of the Mankis and Mundas to certain Mohammedans, Sikhs and Hindus. Twelve villages belonging to Sing Rai Manki and Mohan Manki, proprietors of Silgaon, and eleven other villages had been granted to some Sikhs.[23] Moreover, non-tribal merchants used forcibly to take away all their iron and indignantly throw into their baskets only two pice for each seer of iron taken, although the women would protest that the iron was worth considerably more.[24] Economic injustice was coupled by dishonour done to tribal ladies. It was said that one of the outsiders abducted and dishonoured the wife of Surja Munda of Bandgaon.[25] All these roused great indignation amongst the tribesmen both of Singhbhum and Ranchi. They began to feel that 'their lives are of no value, and being of one caste, let us stand fast to each other and commence to plunder, murder and loot'.[26] They then joined hands to strike against the common enemies.

Though the period from 1821 to 1831 appeared on the surface to be a decade of seeming inactivity and tacit submission by the Hos to inequities, insults and injuries hurled upon them one above the other, it was in reality a period of preparation for a fresh fight greater in magnitude and intensity than the earlier attempt at driving away the foreigners. It was indeed a lull before a storm. So, when the time was deemed ripe to strike against the forces of exploitation there was no dearth of men to swell the army of liberation. The glory of contributing the principal leaders goes to Singhbhum, wherefrom brave men like Topa Suyu, Soma Munda, Surja Munda, Bind Rai, Kate Sardar and Khandu Pater started the operations which were to extend not only throughout the district of Singhbhum but in the Munda land of the district of Ranchi where too there was seething discontent. This discontent took the shape of a rising which spread throughout the length and breadth of Singhbhum, the fringes of the state of Mayurbhanj and the whole of Chotanagpur. The annals of 'the bursting of a fire that had long been smouldering' would have been written in letters of gold but for the lack of persons who could have viewed it with the proper perspective. The accounts available so far are, however, to be found in the shape of letters and documents written by British officers who had invariably termed this heroic struggle for freedom as a campaign for plunder and pillage.

NOTES AND REFERENCES

1. Letter of E. Roughsedge to G. Swinton, Secretary to the Government dated 17 February 1821. para 5.
2. Letter of E. Roughsedge to G. Swinton, 7 August 1821 paras 4-5 (SWFPDR, Vol. 29 BSA), Translation of an Urzee from Rattan Singh dated 13 Magh and received by Roughsedge on 13 February 1821 (SWFPDR, Vol. 27, BSA).
3. Roughsedge to Swinton, 17 February 1821, para 2.
4. Translation of a letter from Chaitan Singh, Thakur of Kharsawan, dated 27 Magh and received by Major Roughsedge on 10 February 1821 (SWFPDR, Vol. 27, BSA); Roughsedge to Swinton, 17 February 1821.
5. Translation of a letter from Raja Ghanashaym Singh dated 25 Magh or 11 February received by Roughsedge on 21 February 1821; A letter from the Dak writer in charge of the stages on Captain Jackson's Road (SWFPDR, Vol. 27 BSA); Translation of an Urzee from Rattan Singh; Translation of a letter from Chaitan Singh; Roughsedge to Swinton, 17 February 1821, para 1.
6. Translation of a letter from Chaitan Singh; Translation of an Urzee from Rattan Singh; Translation of an Urzee from Rattan Singh, received by Roughsedge on 15 February 1821.
7. Roughsedge to Swinton, 17 February 1821, para 8.
8. Translation of a letter from Ghanashyam Singh to Roughsedge; Roughsedge to Swinton, 1 March 1821 (SWFPDR, Vol. 28, BSA).

9. Translation of a letter from Chaitan Singh.
10. Roughsedge to Swinton, 6 March 1821 (SWFPDR Vol. 28, BSA).
11. Roughsedge to Lt.Col. Richards, 22/23 March 1821 (SWFPDR, Vol. 28, BSA).
12. *Ibid.*
13. Roughsedge to Richards, 29 April 1821 (SWFPDR, Vol. 29, BSA).
14. Richards to Roughsedge, 17 April 1821 (SWFPDR, Vol. 29, BSA).
15. Roughsedge to Richards 29 April 1821.
16. Roughsedge to Swinton, 26 April 1821 (SWFPDR, Vol. 29, BSA).
17. Roughsedge to Swinton, 30 April 1821 (SWFPDR, Vol. 29, BSA).
18. O'Malley, *Bengal District Gazetteers*, p. 35.
19. *Ibid.*, p. 34.
20. Though barter was the dominant mode, a few years later we learn that the Hos were gradually 'getting pretty well acquainted' with money. Tickell, 'Memoir'; pp. 804-6.
21. Hunter, *Imperial Gazetteer*, Vol. XII, p. 533; O'Malley, *Bengal District Gazetteer*, p. 34.
22. Roughsedge wrote 'Each village has one or more hereditary headman called Moondha or Mankee whom the rest obey more through prescription and attachment...than fear, for no means enforcing of authority are apparent.' Roughsedge to Metcalfe, 9 May 1820, para 19.
23. Roy, *The Mundas and their Country*, Calcutta, 1912, p. 202.
24. *Ibid.*, pp. 203-4.
25. O'Malley, *Bengal District Gazetteers*, p. 35.
26. Roy, *The Mundas and their Country*, p. 201

4

The Second Struggle and Aftermath

The trend of subsequent events leading to the subjugation of Ho lands by the British in 1837 is to be judged from different angles of vision. On the one side the astute British having stationed their garrisons at strategic places like Chakradharpur, Kat-Karanjia and Bamanghaty, were watching the situation and gaining time to strike the fatal blow at the indomitable *Larka* elements with the help of either the Mahapater or Mahapatra of Bamanghaty, who had been defying the authority of the ruler of Mayurbhanj, or by the ruler himself if he were successful in quelling the former. Another side of the picture would show Mahapater of Bamanghaty who was merely an officer of the Maharaja[1] attempting at overthrowing the Maharaja of Mayurbhanj to establish himself as an independent ruler of several *pirs, viz.* Thai, Bharbharia, Lalgarh and Aula of the district of Singhbhum and a part of the territory of Mayurbhanj. It must have been irritating for the Raja of Mayurbhanj who considered the Mahapater not as his vassal but a mere servant, as his *sarbaraharkar*. He was manoeuvring matters in such a manner as to be in the confidence of the British whom he sometimes helped against the *Larkas* and of the *Larkas* themselves whom he wanted to gain over in totally ousting the imposter of Bamanghaty who was openly helping the British in fighting the *Larkas*. Major Roughsedge wrote "The detachment near Bamanghatee—Kat-Karanjia will ensure the safety of Jackson's Road, give effect to the new relations established between the Zeemindar of the former place and the Lurka of Toeepeer (Thai pir), Burburea (Bharbharia) and Lollgur (Lalgarh) and Onla (Aula) and enable the Ex-killedar to establish himself at Jeyunt-Gurh (Jaintgarh)."[2]

The confusion was further confounded due to the clash of vested interests among local chieftains. The relationship between the rulers of Mayurbhanj and Seraikella had become strained over Kuchang which the former wanted to recover from Ajambar Singh, the ruler of Seraikella.[3] There was boundary dispute between the ruler of Seraikella and Madhu Das Mahapater.[4] In their mutual relationship the Seraikella chief, however, buried their differences and assisted the Mahapater in his conflict with the Raja of Mayurbhanj.[5] But the situation became complicated beyond solution when the local chieftains began to instigate the tribals against each other. Of the four Ho *pirs* referred to above, the Mahapater was able to win over the Lalgarh and Aula people[6] while the other two were gained over by the Mayurbhanj chief by promising them their lands rent free and allowing them the freedom of plunder to them.[7] The Raja of Mayurbhanj assembled the Hos of Jas *pir* and Bharbharia *pir* to induce them to attack and destroy all the villages of Seraikella chief in Kuchang.[8] Moreover, the Rajas of Singhbhum and Mayurbhanj incited Bamanghaty Hos to launch an attack on the villages belonging to the Raja of Seraikella. Incursions were in fact made by the *Larka* Hos upon villages in Tamar and Dhalbhum in January 1836.[9] On the other hand, the Raja of Mayurbhanj complained of two of his villages being attacked by Ajambar Singh, when Madhu Das Mahapater had actually made the attack with the help of the Lalgarh people.[10]

The last element in this confusing political chess board was however the upsurge of discontent which was burning in the remotest hamlets of the wilds of Singhbhum where the brave men were preparing to deal final blow on all intruders who intended to soil the sanctity of their sacred land and the silence and peace of their sylvan solitude. The alien intruder did not deem it wise to face this noble rage of the primitive men who were driven to such despair as had infused in them the grim determination to face even complete annihilation if such contingency arose. Thus the situation was that the British thought it wise to wait for the opportune moment to take action. The interim period was utilized by them in setting one party against the other till all of them were exhausted and rendered weak, the typical British policy to which the local elements fell a helpless prey.

The Ho was depicted by the British in the vilest colours as a savage inclined to commit robbery, arson and murder. Gilbert observed 'It…being expedient to conciliate as much as possible the wild and savage Toeepeer Koles, etc.'[11] This statement amply reveals not only the motive of the writer to vilify the Hos but also the dubious attitude of British officers of the time who would fain conciliate the Ho at any cost. Their oft-repeated claims of maintaining peace in the district and their contention that the Hos, if left to themselves, would prove definite menace to the peace of the district and the well-being of its inhabitants were specious arguments at the justification of their intrusion into and interference with the affairs of other people. The intention of the Company government in the Ho and Munda lands was to have an effective control in order to protect their vested interests in Orissa and to have a direct line of communication between their headquarters at Calcutta and Cuttack in Orissa.[12] Creating grounds for insinuations against their opponents and subsequent aggression had been the patent British policy.

By the third week of March 1832 the Hos were in action. This was the first of the series of heroic acts of the *Larkas* which later on earned the name of the 'Second Kol Rebellion'. This apparently detached action in the southern most extremity of the district of Singhbhum and the borders of the state of Mayurbhanj was one of the presages of the great flame that was to flare up in no time throughout the length and breadth of the areas inhabited by the Hos, the Mundas and the Oraons. Simultaneously with this was the action taken by the men from Porahat who assisted the Mundas in extirpating from their part of the country some undesirable external elements.

The spirit of insurrection had already spread like wild fire and no amount of discretion and calculations on the part of the British could avoid it. Bamanghaty and its neighbourhood were partly desolated by the Hos of Thai and Bharbharia *pirs*. The *Dak* was spared at first but from the middle of April 1832 it was no longer immune. G. Stockwell, Superintendent of Tributary Mahals, Cuttack, reported the incident as also the implications thereof. On 3 April 1832 he was requested by the Company government to ascertain the real cause with the words—'If your information on these points should at present be imperfect, you will be pleased to omit no particular means of fully ascertaining the real circumstances and to lay them before Government with the least practicable delay.'[13] The grave concern of the government was obvious and indicative of their keen interest in the affairs of the region which they called the South Western Frontier. At the same time it was not their motive to plunge into direct action as is evident from the letter dated 8 April 1832 in which Stockwell was advised not to come into collision with the insurgents and to requisition force from Midnapur only in case of apprehension of the insurrection spreading so as to affect the tranquillity of British territories.[14]

In the meantime events had taken such a turn as to make it clear that the Hos would not tolerate any interference on the part of either the Mahapater of Bamanghaty or the Maharaja of Mayurbhanj. The question of their owing any allegiance to the Company government did not or could not arise at that time as the British was the third party interfering into local politics. But whether the Hos recognised their right of interference or not the Company administration was determined to make its importance felt by all concerned. We find that Stockwell was proceeding from Cuttack to Baripada with a government treasure and proper escort. This escort was nothing but an army in disguise which might come into action if and when necessity arose. This is further clarified from the request made by him to government to order Col. Doveton to march from Midnapur to Bamanghaty to suppress any disturbance. Obviously the plan was that these two officers should attack the four *pirs*, the centre of disturbances, from opposite directions. The government on 8 April 1832 granted the permission to do so.[15] During the course of his march to Bamanghaty Stockwell found at Juka on 23 April 1832 that the village had been attacked and the *Dak-Chowkie* looted on 10 April 1832. Stockwell wrote to government: 'the efforts made by the Rajah and more especially the Cole tribes render probable the occurrence of rapine unless effectual measures are adopted.'[16] Thomason, the Deputy Secretary to government, on receipt of similar information beforehand had written to Stockwell 'The arrangement made by Major Roughsedge, under which an assessment was fixed on the 4 Peers, and they were assigned to the Bamanghatee Surburakar, is not one which the Government are anxious to uphold if it be obnoxious to the inhabitants.'[17] The contention that the British had the ultimate motive of assuming power on the plea that the Hos felt the authority of local chiefs to be obnoxious is evident from the above statement. It was, therefore, decided that the British army should take effective action.

So Stockwell was advancing towards Bamanghaty, and Col. Doveton was requisitioned to proceed from Midnapur so as to reach Juka where Stockwell would wait for him. On his march through Saranda towards Juka, Stockwell was convinced that the Hos had taken up arms against all intruders and interference of Mahapater of Bamanghaty would be of no avail. It was also clear to him that not even the ruler of Seraikella, who was then deemed to be the most powerful amongst the chiefs of the district of Singhbhum, could effectually control the *Larkas*. The fact is also borne out by Wilkinson's letter in which he observed that not to speak of the local chiefs, even their own *sardars* under whom, Stockwell, in his conciliatory policy, intended to place the Hos so that they might be peaceful, could now prevail upon the *Larkas*, the majority of whom were determined to drive away all foreign elements that might interfere with them in gaining their ulterior motives. Wilkinson further wrote 'The most powerful of the Singhbhum Chiefs is the koour of Seraikella but he is too far removed from them and not sufficiently powerful. I should apprehend to keep them in check. I know not how the plan of governing them by their own Sirdars would answer as proposed by Mr. Stockwell should Government be inclined to make the experiment.'[18]

On 5 May 1832 Col. Doveton joined Stockwell at Juka apprehending a general rising of the Hos. Once again Stockwell tried to conciliate the Hos. With this aim he met some representatives of the Hos of the four *pirs* assuring them of recognition of their independence. But the Hos did not believe him. Naturally an encounter ensued the result of which was the retreat of the troops of Col. Doveton. The reverse was tried to be explained away by the pretext of illness amongst his soldiers. One more cogent fact however deserves special mention in this connection. This was the resignation of Col. Doveton on 1 June 1832.[19] This resignation, along with the well-designed silence regarding the details of the fights, is eloquent of the fact that the results were not favourable to the British. The unassailable Hos had once again made it clear that in the fastnesses of their hills they were indeed unassailable. This was, however, not the first instance of reverse experienced by the British forces. Between January and March 1832, the prowess of the *Larkas* had compelled them to gather all their forces around Jikilata.

In an official report made in January 1832 R. Kean, the Acting Magistrate, stated 'The insurgents are stated variously to amount to from 1,000 to 1,200 men, but they will in all probability have increased by the time your force will have reached them; they are possessed of no arms, but bows, and arrows and axes, in the use of which they are exceedingly expert, and they further possess the advantage of fastnesses of the hills to which they retire, and to dislodge them is a task of great difficulty.'[20] The Munda population on the borders of the Ranchi and Singhbhum districts rose *en masse.* The *Larka* Hos of Singhbhum came to the aid of the insurgents and formed the most formidable division of the rebel army. The insurrection quickly spread over practically the whole of the present district of Ranchi and overflowed into Hazaribagh, the Tori *pargana* of Palamau, and the western portion of Manbhum.[21]

This bravery and strength of the tribesmen convinced the officers of the Company government that the only local body of troops stationed at Ramgarh would be utterly inadequate to cope with the situation. The Ramgarh Battalion was then stationed at Hazaribagh. They immediately took the field and were reinforced as quickly as possible by troops from Barrackpur and Danapur and by the 50th Bengal Infantry, which was on its march from Gorakhpur.[22]

The British soldiers who encamped at village Selda, in *pargana* Sonepur, proved a sorry match for the resourceful *Larka* Hos. It is said that the *Larkas* remained in hiding in *jungly* recesses during the day and came out at nightfall and shot at the British soldiers from behind when the latter would return to their encampments after a day's futile search. The Mundas claimed that all the British soldiers were killed one after another, till at length the Captain had to go back with the severed heads of his soldiers. The Mundas still commemorate in their songs the victories of the *Larkas* in their struggles with the British troops. One such song records:[23]

Telengako jamanjana
Pithouria parganare,
Larakako hundingajan
Goa Balangare,
Mare Hoko tupuingjan
Jikilata pirire.
Mare Hoko mapajan
Ichahurang Dombaghatre.
Telengako haratingjan
Jikilata pirire,
Larakako darijan,
Ichahurang Doobaghatre.

(Translation)

Within Pithouria bounds,
The soldiers mustered strong.
Balanga Goa saw
The fighting *Larkas* throng.
At Jikilata then
The *Larkas'* arrows flew.
At Dombaghat Ich'rung,
Their foes the Hos shot through.
Ah ! then, on Jik'lata field
The soldiers vanquish'd lay.
At Dombaghat Ich'rung
The Larkas won the day.

After subduing the Mundas the Company government turned towards dealing with their brave supporters, the *Larkas*.

About this a chronicler wrote: 'The assistance rendered by them to the Nagpur Kols in the rebellion of 1831-32 was too gross a defiance of the government to escape serious notice.'[24] The British army from southwest was diverted towards Porahat under Captain Wilkinson. From Tamar the Captain went to Selda and then to Porahat.[25] The battle was, therefore, going on at two fronts, one at the northwestern part of Singhbhum and the other on southern end. The problem before the British was not confined to these fronts only for the vast region in between the two frontiers was like a seething cauldron of discontent, disorder, mistrust and a supreme urge for emancipation from the tortures of outside agencies and the intended and unjustifiable intrusion of the alien Company.

The Captain, therefore, deemed it expedient to adopt a policy of conciliation at first and accordingly on 3 April 1833 an agreement was effected between the Raja of Mayurbhanj, the *Sarbarahakar* of Bamanghaty and the representatives of the *Larkas* of the four *pirs*.[26] This was further confirmed at a conference held at Seraikella in the middle of April 1833 where the Raja of Singhbhum, the ruler of Seraikella, the Thakurs of Kharsawan and Kera as well as the Mankis and Mundas of the Ho *pirs* of Singhbhum were present.[27]

The peace thus effected did not however last long. From January 1834 onwards reports poured in that the Hos were once again restive. The Mahapater of Bamanghaty found it impossible to cope with the situation and fervently appealed to the British for the protection of his territories against the in-roads of the *Larkas*. Not only this, the *Daks* were occasionally disturbed.[28] In April 1834, the Mahapater personally appealed to Wilkinson for the favour of assistance in the shape of guards to check the insurgents who had extensively plundered his villages. This invocation of the Mahapater did not, however, meet with the desired response for Wilkinson insisted that the Mahapater should make his own efforts for preserving his territories without any aid from government.[29] About the same time the *Larkas* and Mahapater's caste men the Dhurwas pillaged and plundered several villages of Mayurbhanj Raj. This led to battles between the Raja's troop and the Ho. Ricketts sent orders to the Raja that he should defend his territories himself.[30] The total impression one would gain from the above situation was that the Hos were actively attacking the territories of both the Raja and the Mahapater and also at intervals interfering with the *Dak* of the Company. But even then the Company government did not deem it expedient to take action. And all this was at a time when the British were not engaged in active warfare either in the South-western Frontier or elsewhere. The engagements in the north and northwestern extremities of the said frontier were over by the end of March 1832. This shows that they were apprehensive of the prowess and determination of the *Larkas* with whom they did not like to have an encounter till they were fully prepared. It might as well be due to the fond hope and expectation that the Hos would be exhausted in their struggle against the local chiefs. The continued aggression of the Hos, however, proved that their store of energy was inexhaustible.

Rickets observed: 'The attacks of the Coles are generally sudden and often made at night.'[31] Three days later he wrote again: 'I hear from other quarters that already several skirmishes have taken place and I think there is every prospect of a struggle and considerable bloodshed.'[32] This compelled Master to communicate: 'I again advocate making the Coles independent of both parties—it appears to me the only chance of preserving quiet in future except severely chastising them a measure which I believe unavoidable—necessity alone would make the government resort to.'[33]

The situation demanded the utmost care and precautionary measures before taking final action. The Company government had appointed intelligence agents. One of whom Roop Singh was stationed at Seraikella by Wilkinson. He reported:

> 'Jemadar Mankie, Dubroo Mankie and Matee (Larka Coles) came to me and (I) said to them when the Sahib (Wilkinson) came to Seraikella he desired you to make such arrangements amongst your brethren in the Colan (Kolhan) as would preserve the peace, now the Coles of your peers have joined the Coles of Bamanghatty and plundered the Bamanghatty Country and Jerryepeer, and

> only left Bamanghatty Ghur untouched; you have now come to make a report after the country has been made a waste. In reply to this the three Mankies said that Toosa Sirdar, Kumlo Gwalla's son Cheeta, the pergunnite of Taeepeer (Thoipir), Dussa Boomije and Madoo Boomije of Burburrea (Bharbharia) peer, had.....ordered them to collect all the Moondas and Mankies, consult and plunder the whole of Bamunghatty and so effectually that not a Darrwah (the Mahapater's caste) should remain in the country...they were to attack Echapeer and having got possession of it a stockade should be erected in Keta from whence Koochang could be plundered—Koonjo of Echapeer was to be spared ...they sent arrows to the Coles of undermentioned Peers of Singhbhum, inviting them to come and assist in plundering Bamanghatty, *viz.* Goomlapeer, Cherriepeer, Berudea, Burkela, Jerra Peer, Jamdapeer and Kategur. The message sent with the arrows was that the Coles were to come and plunder Bamunghatty ...On this invitation the Coles all assembled at Birgaboora, the village of Toosa Sirdar in Tacpeer ...On the 6th day the Coles assembled at night and went to Beenjooa and in the morning attacked and burnt the village—killed the Burnaick (a relation of the Serberakar) ...there were 5,000 or 6,000 Coles present in the attack on Beenjooa.'[34]

On receiving the above report Wilkinson was constrained to advise to government on the same day to take adequate measures to suppress the *Larkas* to save the land from their assaults.[35]

These acts of the bravery of the Hos infused similar zeal in the hearts of other tribes like the Santals and the Bhumij. Even the Chuars of Midnapur were now eager to extend their helping hands in the crusade against the foreigners. 22 June 1834 witnessed the attack on the fort of Bamanghaty by an army of one thousand strong under the leadership of Kurro Santal. This army was comprised of men from several tribes, the Santals, the Bhumij and the Hos and would have succeeded in storming the fort but for the unexpected interference of an army from Seraikella. But Seraikella Chief could not protect the Mahapater for all time to come. He was the marked man of the *Larkas* and realising this he was so despondent that he pathetically appealed to Wilkinson on 24 June that the *Larkas* had rendered his position pitiable.[36]

The interference of the Raja of Seraikella at such a crucial moment, when victory was almost in their hands, could not go with impunity, and Kuchang *pir*, under the possession of Seraikella, was threatened. Ajambar Singh, the ruler of Seraikella, was compelled to report that the tribals of Thai and Bharbharia in conjunction with the people of Gumla, Cheri and other *pirs* and Barndia were threatening to attack his territory.[37]

The pitiable appeal of the Mahapater of Bamanghaty coupled with the cry of help from the ruler of Seraikella amply evidenced the supremacy of the Hos before which all the local rulers were compelled to shudder. Obviously the *Larkas* were active throughout the vast area of Singhbhum and the neighbourhood. On 2 July 1834 Roop Singh, the Intelligence Agent to Wilkinson, reported:

> 'The Coles are again collecting in Thae peer. I fancy the Coles will go in great force and attack Bamunghatty...I have sent for Jemadar Mankie and when he comes I will talk to him—I have also to send Dobasheas to Rundoo Pater and Dubroo, and the other Mankies, I will warn them of the consequence of allowing the Coles to go to Bamunghatty ...It appears to me that the Moondas and Mankies are of one mind with the Coles, because they do not forbid the Coles—the Moondas and Mankies do not attend to the advice I give them.'[38]

The Hos were, therefore, unanimous in their resolution of falling upon the Mahapater of Bamanghaty first and then dealing a blow on the ruler of Seraikella. But at Bamanghaty they were to receive the least resistance from the Mahapater who had meanwhile lost every sympathy and hope of assistance from the ruler of Seraikella who was then himself busy defending his own territories. The question of succour from Mayurbhanj could not and did not arise because of the treacherous tendencies of the Mahapater himself. Bamanghaty struggle was now entering the last phase. The pathetic letter of the Mahapater written on 24 June 1834 did not meet with any response form British side and he was left to his own fate. The end came by the last week of August 1834 (the 4 Bhadra 1241) when Bamanghaty Garh and bazar were attacked. He wrote to Wilkinson on the 6 Bhadra 1241 from Dhalbhum garh (Ghatsila) that about ten or twelve hundred Hos, Santals and Bhuiyans attacked the garh. The Hos felt greatly encouraged after achieving a glorious victory in the pitched battle against a regular army at Bamanghaty bazar. They were determined to attack Seraikella.

In the battle several of Mahapater's men were killed and he was compelled to leave all property behind and escape with his women to Dhalbhum. Though Wilkinson received the above letter on 28 August[39] no help came from the British even at Dhalbhum. Mahapater had ultimately to take shelter under the protection of Seraikella as is evident from Ajambar Singh's *Urzee* to Wilkinson.[40] The reason why the Raja of Seraikella afforded protection and shelter to the Mahapater of Bamanghaty after he was driven away in the last week of August 1834 was to establish a post of Dhurwas (Mahapater's kinsmen and caste men) at Tentoposhi near Bamanghaty for attacking the Hos, with the ultimate object of restoring the Mahapater.

The front, at which the Hos proposed to engage the Seraikella forces, was at Icha and Kuchang, the border of Mayurbhanj. The importance of Kuchang to the Hos was its peculiar strategic situation. From Kuchang as their base they could conveniently attack both Seraikella and Dhalbhum and if constrained to retreat they could recede to the territories of Mayurbhanj where the Seraikella chief could not enter. The importance of Kuchang was not unknown to the British either.[41]

This motive of the Hos to invade and possess Kuchang to which, incidentally, the Raja of Mayurbhanj had also laid a claim was interpreted by and explained to the British authorities by the ruler of Seraikella. Amongst all the ruling chiefs of Singhbhum of the time he was probably the shrewdest and most calculating. He intended to smite at both his opponents, the Hos as well as the Raja of Mayurbhanj.

The British officials at this point of time could not adopt a definite policy. On 15 November 1834 Ricketts sought the permission of the government to launch an attack on the Hos both from the north and the south by assisting the Raja of Mayurbhanj between whose areas the *Larkas* had assembled. But the British administration rejected the proposal.[42] On the other hand Wilkinson intended to support the Mahapater of Bamanghaty whose arrogance against the Maharaja of Mayurbhanj and subsequent misfortune was at the instigation of British authorities. Wilkinson proposed to the government on 4 June 1835 that the best policy for the government would be to strengthen the chiefs of Seraikella and Kharsawan as well as the Mahapater.[43] This policy was favourable for the ruler of Seraikella who, with British assistance was determined to establish the Mahapater once again. As against this the Maharaja of Mayurbhanj though out of the picture was expected to be against the ruler of Seraikella.

While the feudal forces and the British were thus busy in achieving their own political ends the situation became critical for them after the attack on Tiring by the Hos on 23 September 1834. Ajambar Singh realized the seriousness of the situation and fervently appealed to Wilkinson for adequate help in the shape of reinforcement and supply of ammunition. To quote 'the whole of the Coles have combined; if assistance be not given to me I shall not be able to defend my country. I have sent my troops to Eechapeer. Pray send me some powder and balls. I am preparing a stockade round Seraikella.'[44]

Wilkinson informed the government about the gravity of the situation. This probably influenced the Company government to direct Ricketts to issue a warning to the Raja of Mayurbhanj apprising him 'of the serious consequences in which he will involve himself if he should allow his troops or the Coles or other persons acting under his authority or in concert with him to commit any act of depredation or aggression within the British territory or in places under British protection ... any attack on the Koour of Seraikella will most probably tend to his own destruction.'[45]

The warning was issued in the shape of a *parwana* dated 14 October 1834. From this *parwana* it is evident that the Hos had already plundered four of five villages.[46] The chief of Seraikella thus succeeded in his motive of alienating the Maharaja of Mayurbhanj from the British. The threat of the Company government to the Maharaja was indicative of the diplomatic success of Seraikella whose aims were threefold:

1. safeguarding himself from any aggression by the Maharaja of Mayurbhanj, being mortally afraid of which he had to take recourse to such subterfuge.
2. fulfilment of his design of apparently reinstating the Mahapater of Bamanghaty but actually diverting the Hos from close proximity of his territory to Tentoposhi to fight the Dhurwa, the so-called supporters of the Mahapater.
3. to secure for himself adequate military aid from the British to fight his enemies.

So far as the first motive is concerned the ruler of Seraikella could but partially achieve his end for, beyond the threat contained in the *parwana* issued by Ricketts on 14 October 1834, the British did not deem it wise to take any measure which might displease the Raja. Subsequent events clearly indicated that the Raja could not after this humiliation be expected to forgive the ruler of Seraikella. An instance in particular was the occupation of Tentoposhi by the *Larkas* of Lalgarh and Aula and the troops of Mayurbhanj in October 1835.[47]

The second design of keeping the Hos off his territory also met with a reversal. The forces of Mayurbhanj and the *Larkas* after taking possession of Tentoposhi in October 1835 again threatened the borders of Seraikella.[48] Wilkinson became apprehensive of another attack on Kuchang and a determined march of the insurgents against the rulers of Singhbhum. So a fresh warning was issued in November 1835 forbidding the Maharaja of Mayurbhanj from associating with the Hos.[49] The third and the last desire of the chief of Seraikella, *viz.* shelter and protection from the aliens against his neighbours and countrymen however met with perfect success not only during that period but for all time to come. Wilkinson requested the government not to take possession of Singhbhum but to consolidate the position of the rulers of Seraikella and Kharsawan and the Mahapater of Bamanghaty so that they could counter the attacks of the *Larkas*.[50] This letter followed the policy which had been adopted times without number by the British, namely interference in the internal matters for the supposed maintenance of peace and order, providing assistance to the rulers and lastly annexing their territories to British empire on the pretext of inefficiency and misgovernance.

The upheaval throughout Singhbum and parts of the country, which the Company government professed to protect, manifested itself in the shape of skirmishes and battles throughout the length and breadth of the country during the period between September 1834 and June 1835. The message of solidarity among the tribesmen was transmitted by carrying the arrow from one end of the Ho-land to the other inviting their brethren to plunge into the battle for freedom to strike at the aliens and all those who assisted them and to spread the slogan 'burn, plunder, murder and eat.' For a certain period the forces pursuing clever designs, machinations and implementation of the policy of divide and rule were brought to a standstill before the desperate attempt of a 'primitive' race for self-preservation.

The British thought it better to use their discretion to avoid a crisis. Though they did not remain silent spectators they could not precipitate action. Even as late as 1836 the policy was to avoid a 'Cole War'. Ricketts wrote 'but it is to be recollected a Cole War will be an exterminating war; it may at least be inevitable but it is to be avoided as long as possible.'[51]

Though painted in the vilest of colours as plunderers and savage marauders, the Hos, the British knew, were actually invulnerable opponents even for the well-organized and mechanized armies of the British Company. The memories of Jikilata were not to be sunk in oblivion so soon. The aliens chose to avoid a direct clash till it became inevitable. But soon the clash became unavoidable, as from June 1835 the Hos mustered strong at strategic places and launched well-planned attacks against their enemies to prevent their being uprooted from their hearth and home. These attacks were termed as cases of dacoities to give the Hos a bad name and to provide the needed pretext to the British to interfere. Even then they dared not immediately meddle with the Hos during the rainy season of 1835 knowing fully well that taking advantage of the weather and the inability of the British forces to penetrate into the impassable regions, the *Larkas* would successfully take them by surprise and beat them fairly and squarely everywhere. It was, therefore, decided, as suggested by Wilkinson, to the government to take action 'during the cold ensuing season, ... for various aggressions into districts under British protection'[52].

There were now two main fronts, *viz.* Sonepur-Tamar front threatening the territories of the servile followers of the British, the Thakurs of Kharsawan and Kera, and secondly, Koochang-Bamanghaty front to terrorise the ruler of Seraikella. The Governor-General-in-Council, therefore, authorised the Ramgarh Battalion and Irregular horse to march into Singhbhum to enable Wilkinson to launch his operations in November 1835. As regards the first front, the Ramgarh Battalion with the followers of the Kuar of Seraikella and the Thakur of Kharsawan proceeded against the Hos and was successful in subjugating them.[53] The report is surely an admission of the fact that the tribals were considered to be so formidable as to necessitate the alliance of the chiefs of Seraikella and Kharsawan. Not only this, the project of raising a confederated army was also envisaged by the Company government to put into practice the proposal of Ricketts to extend a helping hand to the Maharaja of Mayurbhanj with arms and ammunitions for keeping the Hos in subjection.[54]

From Sonepur-Tamar front the army proceeded to the Kuchang front through the territories of the chief of Seraikella, apprehending the Hos of Rajabasa in Charai *pir* and some other *pirs* of Singhbhum.[55] But the problem in Kuchang-Bamanghaty front was not to be settled so easily. Apprising the government of the dire situation Wilkinson wrote 'it ought to be our policy to repress the power of the Coles and prevent their settling in the countries adjoining those they have always occupied.' He further proposed the posting of a permanent force in the centre of the Kolhan *pirs*. He visualised that in spite of the huge expenditure that the government would have then to incur, as against the slender income from revenue, the government might, in the long run, be driven to take this measure because the Dhurwas of Bamanghaty, who interposed between Ghatsila-Dhul and the Cole *pirs* of Singhbhum, had been driven away from their lands and the Hos had taken possession of their territory.[56]

The proposal of Ricketts was to help the Raja of Mayurbhanj with arms and ammunitions to fight against the Hos from the southern end of Bamanghaty area so that they might be encountered from two fronts, namely the northern one of Kuchang by the forces of Seraikella and the English Company and from the south by the Raja of Mayurbhanj. This was thoroughly scrutinized by the Company authorities as is evident from a series of correspondence between Ricketts, Wilkinson and the Secretary to Government as well as the Court of Directors.[57] It was at last found expedient to combine the forces of the ruling chiefs of Singhbhum as well as the Raja of Mayurbhanj with that of the Company so that the indomitable and tenacious Hos might be subjugated. By this time the problem of dealing with the Hos in Sonepur-Tamar front had already been solved. The military activities of the Company and its allies were, therefore, concentrated in and around Bamanghaty. It was planned that the Hos should be crushed from all sides and to help this they should take advantage of the Dhurwas who were living side by side with the Hos.

The forging of united front against the *Larkas* meant a tacit acceptance of the military strength of the tribesmen. Wilkinson made a candid acceptance: 'Neither the Chiefs of Singhbhoom nor the Rajah of Mahurbunje can control the Lurka Coles, within their Estates although they can all command their services by holding out to them hopes of plunder. The Coles without encouragement have always been willing enough to

the British troops already under him 'by an equal number of men from Dinapore as soon as possible.....considering it probable that the Battalion now at Bankura, may be one of the Regiments employed in Singhboom.'[61] The proposal was duly considered by the Governor-General-in-Council on a reference made by the Government of Bengal and was accepted *in toto*.[62]

The Company government had the troops ready for impending action. It was arranged that Captain Wilkinson would start with the regiment at Bankura so as to reach Seraikella by 18 November 1836 to join Col. Richards who had entered Singhbhum with the Ramgarh Battalion. Richards was to be in charge of this operation.[63] The selection of this officer, particularly at this juncture, was in view of the fact that there was none in the British ranks who had better experience of the topography of the operation as also of the nature of the enemy and their tactics of warfare. He was the person who had, during the last British campaign in the year 1821, succeeded in unleashing a reign of terror throughout Kolhan. However, diplomatic precautions had preceded the military operations in the shape of obtaining absolute assurances of loyalty from the chiefs of Seraikella and Porahat and Thakurs of Kharsawan and Kera. These chiefs, and particularly the Raja of Mayurbhanj, were warned 'of the responsibility they will incur in the event of their giving protection to fugitives, or in any manner obstructing our proceedings and a Perwannah... addressed to the Mayurbhanj Rajah by Mr. Ricketts to the same purpose.'[64]

One should however understand that the friendly relations between the British and local chiefs was not based on cordiality and absolute integrity. The cohesion was in fact the result of preservation of mutual interests. It would have been no wonder if this very weapon of the issue of warnings were at a later date, used by the British as a pretext for withdrawing all favours from these chiefs and of assuming control even over their territories. Meanwhile, all the while British agents were at work to create cleavage amongst the Hos of different *pirs* and to win over some Mankis and Mundas by dangling before them the palliatives of remaining in power and in favour.

Another, and a deeper diplomacy, was the success achieved in inducing the chief of Seraikella and the Raja of Mayurbhanj to indulge in blaming one another in connection with interception of mails on Jackson Road.[65] This ploy was employed to end any possibility of mutual goodwill and understanding between these rulers so that they would not unite against British interest under any circumstances.

The operations started in November 1836. While the forces were getting ready to march into Bharbharia and Thai *pirs* Wilkinson sent a deputation delivering a message of warning to the leaders of the *pirs* that in case they failed to deliver insurgent leaders, thirty of Thai *pir* and thirty six from Bharbharia *pir*, the forces of destruction would be let loose on them. The deputation consisted of a few Mankis who had agreed to take upon themselves the humiliating task of working as agents of the aliens. The deputation reached the *pirs* on 21 November 1836 and assured the Hos of the two *pirs* of British protection provided they did not, under any circumstance, obey the orders of any of the chiefs or Raja but strictly observe whatever rules the Company government might frame for their true management. But all these efforts had no effect on the indomitable and stubborn Adibasis who were determined to carry on the struggle at any cost. Wilkinson duly informed the government about the failure of his mission.[66]

In spite of all preparations, the military operations were delayed till 3 December. Those in command of the British forces were hesitant due to the fierce and unbending attitude of the *Larkas*. It was finally decided to carry on a whirlwind campaign of devastation and havoc intended to create horror in the minds of Adibasi population and to drive them to such destitution that if not for fear they should submit at last for sustenance. Not only were the villages burnt, the suspected leaders butchered and the innocent villagers driven away to the hills but all the grain in store was looted or destroyed and the cattle, the very source of agricultural operation of the people, were also taken away. With the zamindari troops who had joined him earlier on his way from Bankura, Wilkinson reached village Ranju on the borders of Thai *pir* on 3 December 1836. The same day Captain Corfield of the 31st Native Infantry together with

300 Seraikella men attacked Pasubera, Kokcho and Poradiha. The brave residents of these villages had assembled at Mahaburu (Maburu) a place four miles from Kokcho to repulse the impending attack of the British forces. The bravery of these men to whom life was of a little value before the cause of freedom however proved futile because of the scanty response from the Mankis and Mundas, who for the sake of remaining in power, persuaded the comparatively timid elements to surrender and actually effected the tame surrender of the Mundas of Iligara, Gitiladar, Roladih and Ganjia before the British forces in the evening of 3 December itself. But there were others before whom the price of liberty was far above the considerations of mere material gain or the humiliating peace and prosperity accruing out of bondage. The hamlet of Durara in the vicinity of Kokcho had the glory of being inhabited by such persons who knew not how to submit before alien invaders. They had to encounter the assault of 2000 zamindari forces under Captain Wilkinson. This force, employed to take active measures against the Hos of Durara and some of the people of Kokcho, indulged in the looting of the grain of the people and consigning Durara to flames. Wilkinson then entered the heart of Thai *pir*. A detachment of the zamindari troops was sent under Lieutenant Jennar to sack the village Binjburu on river Torlo. Here the troops not only looted or destroyed the grain but also slaughtered all the cattle and set fire to all the houses. The village Purnia met with the same fate. These atrocities were perpetrated on the pretext that the inhabitants of these two villages were connected with the raids on Kuchang and Dhalbhum. The horror created by arson, murder and loot by the British troops resulted in the submission of the Mundas and Mankis of Ukumadkam, Tonto and Kheriatangar as also of Pukhuria. The leaders of these villages attended Wilkinson's camp. On 8 December 1836 Angardiha fell, the brave fighters of which village had gathered in the midst of a cluster of hills. Unlike their neighbours of Ukumadkam, Tonto, Kheriatangar and Pukhuria they preferred to fall down fighting than to submit. They were dealt with even more severely.[67]

Even on the face of these devastating counter insurgency operations eight villages of Thai *pir*, namely Ipilsingi, Chimisai, Lupungbasa, Sidma, Papagara, Jangiburu, Panga and Kundrugutu remained unaffected and determined to carry on the fight. The unbending attitude of the inhabitants of these villages forced Wilkinson to change the strategy. He proceeded to Tentera, a village near Ipilsingi, wherefrom he issued a general warning on 15 December 1836 to the inhabitants of these eight villages to the effect that their non-submission would result in utter annihilation. But the Hos turned a deaf ear to these threats. Lieutenant Corfield of the 31st Regiment then attacked the hillside of Ipilsingi just below the Singhasan hills. Villagers responded to this offensive by retreating to Panga to the south of Singhasan range and occupied a strategic position. The situation became so tense that Ramgarh Light Infantry, under Lawrence, had to be requisitioned to occupy the village and subsequently destroy it. All the grain was looted. The untold and unprecedented miseries and insults flung upon the inhabitants of Ipilsingi and Panga struck such a terror in the minds of the Hos of the neighbouring villages that their leaders at last decided to approach Wilkinson with a proposal to stop his incursions. Wilkinson, accordingly, dictated his terms. The surrender could have perhaps been delayed if the British officers had not succeeded in their usual tactics of winning over greedy and power-loving elements amongst the Hos. Wilkinson wrote: 'The Lurkas are evidently much alarmed, and much I attribute to the impression made by the successful affair on the morning of 4th (December) and subsequent hearty co-operation with us, of the Mankis of Cherrai, Goomla and Bhunje (meaning Binj) which had disheartened their brethren of Toeeper.'[68]

Entering Thai *pir* through the territories of the ruler of Seraikella, probably turning southward from the neighbourhood of Icha, Captain Wilkinson had reached Thai *pir*. After the aforesaid operations he moved southeastwards to capture Bharbharia *pir*. The route intended to be followed was from Panga to Butka, Butka to Bhagabila, and then, after crossing the range of hills, dividing Lalgarh and Aula *pirs* on the southern side and Bharbharia and Thai *pirs*, to the north to Angardiha in Lalgarh *pir*. From Angardiha they were to proceed onwards to Dumuria via Majhgaon and later to Balandia. The projected march therefrom was to Gamaria-Jagannathpur and Satbantari whence they would retreat to Gumla *pir* in the vicinity of present Chaibasa.[69]

On 22 December 1836, Wilkinson moved from Bhagabila to Angardiha in Lalgarh. In Angardiha Mundas and four *sardars* of the Lalgarh *pir* surrendered to him. He then procured information about the names and rendezvous of the insurgent *Larkas*. This helped him in apprehending about sixty insurgents. He then moved on 10 January 1837 to Majhgaon, a village of Aula *pir*. Next day several Mundas and three *sardars*, excepting one named Barnda, who provided shelter to many insurgents in his village Ichakuti, submitted. But soon some Mankis of the Kolhan *pirs* of Singhbhum brought him before Wilkinson who put him under restraint. To strike terror in the hearts of these, who had not laid down arms, he then made the exemplary attack and plunder of the village Harruakumar because the Munda of this village had dared defy the repeated orders to surrender. This seemed to unnerve Mundas of other villages also who tendered their submission. All the insurgents save five, were captured and several heads of cattle were also recovered.[70]

On 23 January Wilkinson reached Dumuria in the Barndia division of Jaintgarh. The majority of the Mundas joined him there. Wilkinson asked them to surrender the insurgents in their respective villages and help him in recovering the cattle which had been carried off by the *Larkas* from Keonjhar. But the headmen pleaded their inability as the rebels had escaped to their hideouts in hills and jungles. Meanwhile Capt. Lawrence arrived with his troops to reinforce the army under Wilkinson. On 26 January 1837 Lawrence made a surprise attack on the Barndia *Larkas* and succeeded in capturing many Ho men and women insurgents. An attack on another Barndia booth by Capt. Corfield did not however succeed as the insurgents had meanwhile abandoned the booth on receiving the information of an impending attack. They had left their cattle and grains behind. When Corfield's men tried to carry off the grains, the *Larkas* pounced upon them and killed a few of their enemies. Kunwar Ajambar Singh's troops, accompanying Corfield's detachment, then planned an assault on the Hos. But meanwhile they had again retreated to the safety of hills and jungles. These abortive moves forced Wilkinson to send two parties on 31 January 1837 to comb the adjacent hills and jungles for grains and looted cattle. Though they were able to recover a small portion of grains, they failed to locate the *Larkas*. Next, Wilkinson sent troops of Seraikella and some loyal Hos to search the hills and jungles again. The four-day long operations resulted in the capture of many insurgents, the principal among whom was Jotong, who had killed the camp men of Corfield. The success of the British contingent seemed to unnerve the Mundas of Barndia division who surrendered to Wilkinson.

On 9 February Wilkinson reached Gomaria. At Gomaria the headman surrendered sixteen insurgents. Wilkinson next moved to village Satbantari. All the Mundas of the Satbantari *pir* and the Manki of the Jamda *pir* surrendered to him. Meanwhile, serious sickness broke out among his troops preventing further offensive movement of English contingent. Wilkinson then issued out messages of warning to headmen of Kotgarh and Rengra *pirs* directing them to surrender at either Gumla or Chaibasa. The strength of the British arms and the fear of reprisal in case of recalcitrance naturally created a sense of panic among all those Mundas and Mankis who had evaded submission till then. All the village heads of Rengra, Kotgarh, Aula, Thai, Bharbharia, Lalgarh and Satbantari *pirs*, as well as the Mundas and Naiks of Jaintgarh, the Mankis of the Kotgarh, Jamda, Natua, Saranda and Rengra *pirs* as well as all the Mankis and Mundas of Gumla, Barkela, Charai, Ajodhya, Chainpur, Gopinathpur, Govindpur, Kalinua pirs and Ho pirs and villages under the rulers of Seraikella and Kharsawan approached Wilkinson and surrendered to him. These tribal headmen agreed to obey the orders of the British government only and to pay the *malguzari* at the rate of eight annas per working plough after the ensuing rains to the government.[71]

The British campaign was carried on according to programme and with all the resources at their command. Even then the time involved in reaching their goal proved unexpectedly long. It might be due to dour resistance offered by the Hos and also due to the inaccessibility of the region. Details of these detached encounters have not however been traceable either from the letters of the different officers in charge of the affairs nor are there any traces of reliable stories handed down from generation to generation to acquaint us with the actual happenings. There is, however, nothing much left for surmise because the whole of the military operation was nothing short of constant repetition of plunder and pillage by the British troops as also their usual indulgence in promoting discord between different elements of the population and creation of collaborators in the shape of persons craving for power or wealth. One thing is certain that their progress had never been very smooth. By 14 February 1837 Wilkinson was convinced that there was no apprehension of further risings of the *Larkas*. In self-complacence he communicated the government that 'When the Coles have been brought into good order, and become more civilised which I have no doubt they will be in a few years under judicious management, Government will be amply repaid for any expense.'[72] But he also did not fail to mention that for the preservation of future tranquillity a strong force should be stationed preferably at a position near Seraikella.[73]

The depth of British diplomacy cannot be gauged so easily as this very move is indicative of the underlying policy not only of ensuring safety of the forces from the ferocious Hos so recently subjugated, but also of having some control over neighbouring zamindars whom too in the heart of hearts probably they could not trust.[74]

Be it as it may, the British Captain had to acknowledge the bravery and stubbornness of the Hos as a people and their superiority over their neighbours.[75] This shows that at heart the British had greater respect for the so-called savage than their comparatively civilised neighbours, their faithful feudal allies whom too, they intended to crush, if needs be with the help of Hos. After this victory the civil administration of the area was entrusted with Lieutenant S.R. Tickell who was vested with civil and political powers over the newly carved out territory named as the Kolhan Government Estate, comprising in all 622 villages and 26 *pirs* belonging to the Bamanghaty subdivision and Singhbhum.[76]

NOTES AND REFERENCES

1. Stockwell to Thomason, Deputy Secretary to Government dated 14 April 1832, *vide Memorial of the Mayubhanj State to H.E. the Rear Admiral the Right Honourable Viscount Mountbatten of Burma, Viceroy and Governor General of India and Crown Representative,* Baripada, Mayurbhanj, 1947, p. 29.
2. Roughsedge to Swinton, 16 May 1821 (SWFPDR, Vol. 27, BSA).
3. Government of Bengal, Judicial Department to Court of Directors, East India Company, 6 September 1836, Letter No. 14 of 1836, para 12 (Judicial General Letter to the Court of Directors from 17 March 1835 to 18 November 1836, Vol. 17 (WBSA).
4. Wilkinson to H. Ricketts, Superintendent Tributary Mahals. Cuttack 14 December 1835 (SWFPDR, Vol. 126 BSA).
5. Letter No. 14 of 6 September 1836, paras 5 and 8.
6. *Ibid.*, para 9.
7. *Memorial of the Mayurbhanj State* (henceforth MMS), pp. 32-33.
8. Wilkinson to Ricketts, 18 May 1836, para 3 (SWFPDR, Vol. 126, BSA).
9. Letter No. 14 of 6 September 1836, para 12.
10. Wilkinson to Ricketts, 18 May 1836, para 1.
11. Gilbert to Pakenham, the Commissioner of Cuttack, 31 March 1827, cited in MMS, p. 24.
12. T. Wilkinson to R.D. Mangles, 22 August 1836 (SWFPDR, Vol. 126, BSA).
13. MMS, p. 28.
14. *Ibid.*
15. *Ibid.*
16. *Ibid.*, pp. 29-30.
17. Thomason to Stockwell, 24 April 1832, cited in MMS, p. 30.
18. Wilkinson to Thomason, 6 May 1832 (SWFPDR, Vol. 145, BSA)
19. MMS, pp. 31-32.
20. Roy, *The Mundas,* p. 205.
21. O'Malley, *Bengal District Gazetteers,* p. 36.
22. *Ibid.*
23. Roy, *The Mundas,* 1970, p. 117.

24. Hunter, *The Imperial Gazetteer,* Vol. XII, p. 553.
25. Roy, *The Mundas,* 1912, p. 208.
26. MMS, p. 33.
27. *Ibid.,* p. 35.
28. Wilkinson to Post Master General, 16 March 1834, *vide* MMS, p. 35.
29. Wilkinson to Ricketts, 13 June 1834, *vide* MMS, p. 35.
30. Ricketts to Wilkinson, 21 May 1834, *vide* MMS, p. 36.
31. Ricketts to J. Master, Acting Commissioner of Cuttack, 21 May 1834, cited in MMS, p. 36.
32. Ricketts to Master, 24 May 1834, *vide* MMS, p. 36.
33. Master Ricketts, 3 June 1834, *vide* MMS, p. 37.
34. Urzee of Roop Singh, a Government servant stationed at Seraikella, 13 June 1834 and received on 17 June 1834 (SWFPDR, Vol. 125, BSA).
35. Wilkinson to MacSween, 17 June 1834, *vide* MMS, p. 38.
36. Translation of an Urzee from Madhu Das Mahapater, 24 June 1834 (SWFPDR, Vol. 125, BSA)
37. Translation of an Urzee from Kunwar Ajambar Singh of Seraikella 27 June 1834 (SWFPDR, Vol. 125, BSA).
38. Wilkinson to MacSween, 2 July 1834, Enclosure 8, *vide* MMS, p. 44.
39. Wilkinson to MacSween, 5 October 1834, *vide* MMS, p. 46.
40. *Ibid.,* p. 46.
41. *Ibid.,* p. 48.
42. *Ibid., p.* 50.
43. Letter No. 14 of 6 September 1836, para 26.
44. Translation of an Urzee from Ajambar Singh of Seraikella, 23 September 1834 (SWFPDR, Vol. 125, BSA).
45. MMS, p. 48.
46. *Ibid.*
47. Letter No. 14 of 6 September 1836, para 10.
48. *Ibid.*
49. MMS, p. 51.
50. Wilkinson to Mangles, 4 June 1835, vide MMS, pp. 50-51.
51. Ricketts to Secretary to the Government, 4 June 1836, *vide* MMS, p. 56.
52. Secretary, Military Department, Government of India to Quarter Master General of the Army, 21 September 1836, quoted in MMS, p. 52.
53. Wilkinson to Mangles, 22 August 1836.
54. Ricketts to Secretary to the Government, 8 November 1835, *vide* MMS, p. 51.
55. Wilkinson to Mangles, 22 August 1836.
56. Wilkinson to Mangles, 21 December 1835, vide MMS, p. 53.
57. MMS, pp. 53-55.
58. Wilkinson to Mangles, 22 August 1836, paras 42, 44-45.
59. *Ibid.,* para 47.

60. *Ibid.*, paras 48-49.
61. *Ibid.*, paras 55-58.
62. Macnaghten to Mangles, 30 October 1836, para 5, *vide* MMS, p. 60.
63. Hunter, *The Imperial Gazetteer of India*, Vol. XII, p. 253.
64. Wilkinson to Mangles, 5 November 1836, paras 4-5 (SWFPDR, Vol. 126, BSA)
65. Ricketts to Secretary to the Government in the Judicial Department, 13 November 1836, cited in MMS, p. 62.
66. Wilkinson to Mangles, 30 November 1836, para (SWFPDR, Vol. 126, BSA).
67. Wilkinson to Secretary Government of Bengal, 9 December 1836, *vide* MMS, pp. 63-64.
68. *Ibid.*, 18 December 1836, *vide* MMS, p. 64.
69. *Ibid.*, 7 January 1837, *vide* MMS, p. 65.
70. *Ibid.*, 7 and 22 January 1837, *vide* MMS, p. 65.
71. *Ibid.*, 14 and 28 February 1837, *vide* MMS, pp. 65-66.
72. *Ibid.*, 28 February 1837.
73. *Ibid.*, 14 February 1837.
74. *Ibid.*, 28 February 1837.
75. *Ibid.*
76. *Ibid.*; Wilkinson to Tickell, 13 May 1837, paras 1-2 (SWFPDR, Vol. 231, BSA).

5

The Alien Tightens His Grip

The British claimed that the conquest of Kolhan was not a spontaneous act of imperialism but was imposed on them. The reason as observed by Wilkinson was 'for the purpose of taking charge of Cole peers in Singhbhum and Bamanghatty, which have been brought under the direct management of the British Government, owing to the inability of the Chiefs of these Estates, which they were to keep in control the Lurkas, the inhabitants of those peers.'[1] To this was added the benevolent gesture of the British in providing justice to the tribals. Wilkinson wrote 'I have found from experience with respect to all the Zamindars... that justice is never done by them and non-investigation of complaint and withholding redress may lead the aggrieved, more particularly the Coles, to take the law into their own hands.'[2]

However, this was not the simple act of altruism but was motivated by vested interests. The British had carved out this precious possession to serve as a connecting link between their possessions in Bengal and Orissa. This alone could prompt the British to compromise with the economic loss which its subjugation immediately brought for them. Wilkinson pointed out that 'this, of course, would fall short of extra expenses attending the arrangement, but in comparison to the advantages of preserving order and tranquillity in a country so near the seat of Government and immediately bordering on the productive provinces of Bengal and Orissa.'[3] Not this alone the British planned to utilize the *Larkas*, whom they identified as the 'powerful people', to 'overawe, or punish if necessary neighbouring Zamindars, who might venture to set

Government at defiance.'[4] With these motives the Company government laid the foundation of the administration which was directed at tightening the shackles of bondage round the people of Singhbhum.

Kolhan formed part of the administrative unit known as the South West Frontier Agency which was carved out of the non-regulation areas of Chotanagpur division by Regulation XIII of 1833. The administrative head was called the Assistant to the Political Agent of SWFA with headquarters at Chaibasa. The first to occupy this office was Lt. Tickell.[5] The Assistant held wide powers in revenue and judicial matters and in the maintenance of the law and order, subject to the general supervision and control of the Political Agent. The Rules for the administration of Criminal Justice were framed in 1837 by the government. These empowered the Assistant to receive and investigate all complaints, charges and information in regard to crimes committed or misdemeanours shown within his area and after conviction to punish by fine upto rupees fifty or imprisonment for a maximum period of two years. However, decisions taken by him were again subject to revision on a petition of appeal to the Agent who could confirm, annul or modify such orders.[6] He could also sentence an offender to imprisonment for a period of five years. But any such sentence beyond two years was liable to final approval and confirmation by the Agent for which the Assistant was required to forward all relevant papers in original to the Agent. The Agent could confirm, annul or modify the orders of the Assistant or he could try the case himself.[7] In discharging his duties the Assistant was required to take help of the Mankis or their assistants or to establish direct contact with the people and not to solely depend on the *Dobhasias*.[8] He was instructed to be strict in apprehending thieves and plunders with the help of the Mankis, their assistants, and Mundas.[9]

The Political Agent had powers to exercise control over the *Nizamat Adalat* or appellate court of criminal jurisdiction and over his Assistant and other subordinates. He was empowered to award the death sentence. Any award exceeding fourteen years of rigorous imprisonment by him was however required to be approved and confirmed by the Governor of Bengal for which the Agent had to submit the report of the proceedings.[10] He could impose a fine up to five hundred rupees, beyond which he was liable to report the circumstances of the case to the government for confirmation.[11] The Agent was empowered to exercise the same powers in awarding rewards for apprehending proclaimed offenders as were vested in the Commissioner of Circuit in the Regulation Provinces.[12] All sentences awarded by the Agent or final orders issued by government were to be implemented by him in the same manner as were done by the Sessions Judge.[13] The Agent could call for the proceedings of the cases decided by the Assistant and to issue orders thereon either in mitigation or remission of punishment as he deemed fit.[14] He was required to submit to the higher authorities the periodical reports containing the number and nature of crimes committed, number of persons apprehended, convicted and sentenced, the nature of punishment awarded, the numbers of prisoners in confinement under examination as well the quantum of fines decided by his and his Assistant's courts and contingent expenses.[15] The above rules remained operative in Kolhan till the enforcement of the Criminal Procedure Code Act XXV in 1864.[16]

Captain Wilkinson framed a few simple rules in 1837-38 for the administration of Civil Justice.[17] In all civil cases the Assistant was required to make as much use as possible of *panchayats* taking care to select the most respected and intelligent amongst the Hos to compose the *punch*. He was also enjoined to take written engagements from the parties binding themselves to abide by any decision the *punch* might take. When the *panchayat* had come to a decision it should invariably be recorded in Assistant's office. After it had been written and the *punch* had affixed their marks to it, the Assistant should see it carried to execution.[18]

The Company government legalised the indigenous village organisation. Wilkinson accorded a legal status to the Mankis. The larger Kolhan *pirs* were subdivided. A *pir* was placed under the jurisdiction of a Manki.[19] It generally comprised villages not exceeding twenty.[20] A Manki was chosen mainly on the basis of the influence he wielded in his locality and his acceptability among the people of the villages therein. The Manki was empowered to select one or more persons for his assistance from amongst the Mundas and raiyats of villages within his area.[21] Regarding the succession to the office of Manki, J.H. Crawford, the Agent, ruled in 1851 that this office was neither purely elective nor strictly hereditary. The person with the greatest local influence was to be considered the best qualified to succeed on the death or dismissal of a Manki. But if he had no direct heir, a member of his family, could succeed on the death of a Manki when the deceased had discharged his duties creditably. The minor heir of a competent Manki could also be his successor. In that case, one of his qualified relatives was allowed to act on his behalf till he came of age.[22]

The Mankis, their assistants and Mundas were armed with police as well as revenue powers. A Manki was made the chief police officer of his area while a Munda functioned as his subordinate. Each *pir* thus became virtually a police circle with the Manki as the sub-inspector and the Munda was like the head constable of the regular police.[23] The *pir* and village heads were not independent 'to act on any orders they may receive, except communication to them by you (Assistant) directly or through the Mankies or their assistants.'[24] Moreover, by the terms of agreements between the Mankis and the Company government they were definitely instructed to report to the Agent of any such attempt on the part of his non-aboriginal neighbours. The *patta*, given in the year 1838 to Jamadar Manki of Asura by Lt. Tickell, contained: 'If any order comes to you from any Raja, Babu or Bhaiya you should not according to your promise, carry it out but will produce before me the man who comes with such orders from them. You will carry out all orders. You will receive a separate "Patta" that you will get one-tenth of the total revenue of your Ilaka.' Not only this, there was a threat of punishment recorded in the same *patta* with the words 'If you show negligence in the discharge of your duties this "Sanad" will be taken away from you and given to another man.'[25]

The conquest of Kolhan thus introduced the British administration into the area in which indigenous institutions were integrated merely as a cog to consolidate and penetrate British control over this area. In the name of providing legitimacy, it succeeded in ensuring absolute subservience of the Manki, the headman and leader of the community. A Ho who could scarcely perceive how his independence was being ebbed away through the agency of his own tribal leader whom the glamour of power and wealth had attracted towards the foreigner. The imperialist dragnet was further spread to directly involve common man through the land revenue administration.

In 1821 the British had introduced in the Ho land the rather unconventional method of paying a tribute of eight annas for each working plough or yoke of oxen to the local chieftains. The same practice was continued after 1837 with the difference that the beneficiary became the Company government instead of the chiefs. It was decided that the land requiring from 4 to 5 *khundees* of seed *dhan* to sow it, should be considered one plough of land and the number of ploughs in a village cultivating the lands of that village at 8 annas per plough and the quantity of seed sown by non-resident cultivators of the village lands at 8 annas per (each *khundee* of 20 *pies*) 5 *khundees* of seeds, would give the actual village assessment.[26] The Assistant was directed to ascertain, with the help of the Mankis and Mundas, after the rains were over, the number of resident cultivators in each village and the ploughs employed by them as well as the number of non-resident cultivators and the extent of land cultivated by them.[27] After the assessment the Mundas were instructed to collect the rent and pay the amount to the Assistant directly or to him through the Manki.[28] The *pir* and village heads received a portion of the rent as remuneration for collecting rents and performing police duties.[29] The rates were one-tenth and one-sixth respectively for the Mankis and Mundas. In 1837-38 the net rent collected stood at Rs. 5108-1-8.[30] In 1854 a re-assessment was made when the quantum of rent was enhanced to rupee one and the ryots were given *pattas* for twelve years. This raised the amount collected to Rs.17,700.[31]

After the introduction of the above changes the British administrators believed that by having control over the Mankis and Mundas they would be able to shape things according to their own designs. The apparent calm in the land misled them to think that the quiet meant contentment and final surrender of the *Larkas* to the benevolent British rule. Dalton observed: 'During this period the revenue was paid with the utmost punctuality. The area of cultivation rapidly increased, and there was every reason to suppose that the people were contented and making fair progress in civilization and prosperity.'[32] But this apparent calm was not in reality the mark of surrender. The rude rebuff came in 1857 when the tribal people of Singhbhum joined hands with non-tribals to launch the crusade against the foreigners for the reassertion of the rights of the children of the soil. This time their leader was Raja Arjun Singh of Porahat. It may be pointed out in this connection that Wilkinson had instructed his assistant in 1837: 'Care must be taken to prevent the Rajah of Singhbhoom, Kooar of Seraikella, Thacoor of Khursawa, Mohurbhunje Rajah and other Baboos from intriguing with the Coles and if at any time you should discover that any of the Coles within your district should have joined any of them in military operations against their own Zamindars or against each other you must take immediate steps to bring them to punishment.'[33] The British policy of isolating the tribal people from the local chiefs and non-tribals did not seem to succeed as the events during 1857-58 showed.

NOTES AND REFERENCES

1. Wilkinson to Tickell, 13 May 1837, para 1.
2. *Ibid.*, para 16.
3. Wilkinson to Mangles, 23 February 1837, para 10.
4. *Ibid.*, para 9.
5. Wilkinson to Tickell, 13 May 1837, para 1.
6. Rules for the administration of Criminal Justice in the Kolhan of Singhbhum and Bamunghatty under the Political Agent of the South Western Frontier, dated 6 June 1837, No. 615, para 2 (SWFPDR. Vol. 231, BSA).
7. *Ibid.*, para 3.
8. Wilkinson to Tickell, 13 May 1837, para 5.
9. *Ibid.*, para 8.

10. Rules, para 1.
11. *Ibid.*, para 15.
12. *Ibid.* , para 11.
13. *Ibid.*, para 13.
14. *Ibid.*, para 14.
15. *Ibid.*, para 15.
16. W.W. Hunter, *A Statistical Account of Bengal*, Vol. XVII, p. 75.
17. Wilkinson to Tickell, 13 May 1837, para 28.
18. *Ibid.*, para 21.
19. *Ibid.*, para 4.
20. Governor-General's Agent to Lt. Tickell, 10 December 1838, para 2, *vide* P.C. Roy Choudhury, *Singhbhum Old Records*, Patna, 1958, pp. 12-3.
21. Wilkinson to Tickell, 13 May 1837, para 4.
22. Governor General's Agent to Lt. Haughton, 1st class Assistant Agent, Singhbhum Division, 17 March 1851, *vide* Roy Choudhury, *Singhbhum Old Records*, pp. 31-34.
23. Hunter, *A Statistical*, p. 118.
24. Wilkinson to Tickell, 13 May 1837, para 6.
25. A.D. Tuckey, *Final Report on the Resettlement of the Kolhan Government Estate in the District of Singhbhum 1913-18*, Patna, 1920, p. 13.
26. Wilkinson to Tickell, 13 May 1837, para 29.
27. *Ibid.*, paras 29 and 31.
28. *Ibid.*, para 30.
29. *Ibid.*, para 33.
30. Hunter, *A Statistical*, pp. 82 and 87.
31. Dalton, *An Introduction*, p. 183. See also Bradley Birt, *Chota Nagore*, p. 94.
32. Dalton, *An Introduction*, p. 183.
33. Wilkinson to Tickell, 13 May 1837, para 24.

6

A Brave Tribe Rallies Round a Brave Raja

The year 1857 witnessed the first struggle of our independence which staggered the machinery of British administration in India both supreme and local. This outbreak, which lasted barely for a year in other parts of the country, continued in the district of Singhbhum for a longer period. For the British it meant anxiety, uneasiness and danger. This found expression in Lieutenant Governor Sir Frederick Halliday's letter, where he wrote that in fact no division in the whole of Bengal had been subjected to such a continued and prolonged disturbance as Chotanagpur.[1] The division of Chotanagpur extended to the whole length of the Grand Trunk Road from Raniganj to Sherghati covering a distance of about 200 miles with scattered garrisons of Indian troops. These forces had almost in every instance mutinied openly in which they got the support of the local chiefs who almost in every instance collected the people round them.

The news of the rising of the garrison of the Indian troops at Danapur under the leadership of the hoary-headed octogenarian, the 'remarkable land owner Kunwar Singh', reached Hazaribagh on 30 July 1857. The detachment of the 8th Native Infantry at once mutinied and drove their military and civil officers out from the station.[2]

News at this time was spreading like wild fire and that of the rising of the Hazaribagh unit of the Ramgarh Battalion reached Doranda sometimes after 30 July 1857. All that later happened at Chaibasa during 1857 was dependent on synchronous events in other parts of the country and especially at Doranda. The chronicle of the happenings in Singhbhum of the time need, therefore, to be preceded by a narration of the rising at Doranda.

Soon after the soldiers at Ramgarh, Hazaribagh and Doranda had taken up arms against their alien masters the detachment of the 8th Native Infantry of the Ramgarh Light Infantry Battalion plundered the treasury, released the prisoners and left the station. The officer commanding Doranda cantonment sent Lieutenant Graham with thirty horsemen of the Ramgarh Irregular Cavalry, two companies of Ramgarh Battalion and two guns to Hazaribagh in order to quell the rebellion and to disarm the rebels. The officer commanding had not an inkling that the troops sent by him might not remain loyal. On the way Graham was informed by Captain Oakes that the rising at Hazaribagh was not a mere local mutiny, that the rebels had seized the guns and camp equipages and they were on their march to spread the wave of insurrection throughout. Such a mighty blaze could hardly be covered and the authorities could not keep the events screened from the public eyes. On the way to Hazaribagh Graham's own infantry rebelled, seized the guns, ammunitions as well as four elephants which were the private properties of Captain Dalton. The rebels then marched back to Ranchi. Graham could not control the situation. Before this news reached Ranchi, Captain Dalton and other European officers had abandoned that station. The armed insurgents, on their march back, found that there was none to oppose them and accordingly they took possession of the treasury and released the prisoners from the jail. They were then joined by the troops stationed at Doranda. On this occasion, according to Col. Malleson, the armed rebels fired cannon at the Church and burnt down bungalows.[3] This appears to be apparently incorrect since far deeper emotions of patriotism and honour lay at the root of their actions. So to impute the motives of pillage and plunder to their noble rising would be nothing short of slander and vilification by the foreigner. Had there been the slightest opposition against their march by the British the question of retaliation or vengeance could have cropped up. But since there was none the so-called charge against the rebels having committed acts of atrocity does not stand, although many chroniclers so often resorted to it.

The stations of Ranchi and Doranda were the most important stations in the division. The first was then the seat of the Agent to the Governor-General-in-Council and the second the headquarters of a garrison of no mean importance. These fell in the hands of the insurgents without any bloodshed. Apprehending a more serious insurrection, which they feared, might adversely affect the civil population, Captain Dalton and other Europeans left their stations without caring to protect the residents whose lives and properties they had professed to safeguard.[4] So when the Indians were left to their own fates they had one obligation left, namely to join the insurgents who had raised arms against foreign rule. This represented, to quote the words of Sir Lepel Griffin, an experienced Anglo-Indian administrator of the time, 'an unprogressive, selfish and commercial system of administration.' And this is one of the reasons which went to make this a struggle for independence against obnoxious foreign domination in which all sections of the local population participated. The sepoy mutiny was soon converted into a civil rebellion in the hills and dales of Chotanagpur.

The news of the rebellion of the troops stationed at Doranda reached Chaibasa sometime on 3 or 4 August 1857. Referring to the reaction of the news in the minds of the inhabitants of Singhbhum Captain Dalton wrote 'When it became generally known at Chyebassah that Ranchee had been abandoned by the Officers of the Commission, coupled with the sudden disappearance of their own officer, there was, as a matter of course, considerable excitement, and it is stated that a Proclamation was issued announcing that Urjoon Singh was the ruler of the country.'[5] Major Sissmore was the Principal Assistant Commissioner in charge of the District of Singhbhum. On hearing of the disturbances at Hazaribagh and Ranchi, he thought it wise to abandon the station and to first place himself under the protection of Chakradhar Singh, the Raja of Seraikella and then retreat to Raniganj with an escort provided by the Raja.[6]

After the abrupt departure for Seraikella on 5 August Major Sissmore issued *perwanahs* through the Raja of that place calling upon all the principal chiefs in the district to send men for the protection of the Sadar Station. According to Lushington the detachment of the Ramgarh Battalion stationed at Chaibasa did not revolt before 3 September 1857. If that was so there was no reason for Major Sissmore to leave the station abruptly. On the contrary, there is evidence to conclude firstly, that Major Sissmore's departure on 5 August 1857 was not under peaceful circumstances and secondly, that the rebellion at Chaibasa took place on 5 August 1857 itself.[7] I quote Col. Malleson in support 'At Purulia and at Chaibasa the other posts in Chutia Nagpur occupied by native troops, scenes had taken place similar to those enacted at Ranchi and Hazaribagh. On the 5th August, the sepahis of the Ramgarh battalion, stationed at those places, mutinied, plundered the treasury, released the prisoners and sacked the private houses of the Europeans.'[8]

We have yet another source which does not only corroborate the view expressed by Col. Malleson so far as the date of the revolt is concerned but also further supports that Chaibasa, the Sadar station of the district of Singhbhum was not then in British occupation nor was in the occupation of the ruler of Seraikella under whose care the charge of the station was committed. W. Grey, Secretary to the Government of India, wrote: 'On the 28th August, Lieutenant Birch was ordered to reoccupy Chaibasa.'[9] These two sources perhaps indicated that rebellion might have started at Chaibasa days before the generally accepted date of 3 September.

Prisoners released from jail and others joined the rebellion started by the sepoys of the Ramgarh Battalion at Chaibasa. Here Nafar Mukhtar, an employee of Raja Arjun Singh of Porahat, was actively engaged in summoning the Hos, explaining to them that the English had abandoned the 'Country', and that it had become the property of the Raja. A letter was subsequently found in Porahat from this man to the Raja, inviting him to come to Chaibasa and take possession of the town.[10] On 10/12 September Sham Karan Singh, the agent of Arjun Singh, made a formal proclamation that 'The people belong to the Almighty, the Country belongs to the King and the ruler thereof is Maharaj Urjoon Singh.'[11]

Before actually plunging headlong into this deadly strife Raja Arjun Singh summoned the Mankis and Mundas of the district in a meeting to feel the pulse of the people. The Mankis and Mundas were the representatives of the tribesmen in the district and they wielded enormous influence over their people. They solemnly took an oath to support the Raja in his war against the British.[12]

The sadar sub-division of the district of Singhbhum was mostly inhabited by the Adibasis who were not oblivious of their glorious deeds only two decades back and who could hardly bear the yoke of British rule any longer. Their inherent spirit of independence once more manifested itself when they thought it proper to join *en masse* with the forces of liberation. The trend of subsequent events clearly showed that they earnestly felt the necessity of overthrowing a foreign government which was imperceptibly crippling them and bringing on them an economic slavery and political servitude.

To recapitulate, for a score of years immediately preceding this rebellion the aliens had sought to brow bit the proud race by demonstration of force and acts of unparalleled atrocity. For the time being they had been quelled but they always cherished the idea of regaining their erstwhile glory should chance and opportunity come in their way. The time was now ripe for the Adibasi to hit back the cruel conqueror and they did not lag behind in availing of the chance offered by the mutinous army and the Raja of Porahat in whom they could find a true leader.

The rebel sepoys were also seeking a leader and they too discovered in the Raja one who could rise to the occasion and carry them through. This trust was duly supported by messages from Doranda where the sepoys had taken up arms. The Raja also sent one Mookond Roy with a letter to Thakur Bishwanath Sahi of Barkagarh, one of the rebel leaders at Ranchi.[13] As stated earlier the troops stationed at Chaibasa released the prisoners from jail and left Chaibasa. The rebels came at a place called Doomra where the Hos stopped them. The Hos, however, allowed the rebels to proceed when they were informed that it was Raja Arjun Singh's desire that they should be allowed to proceed to the Char opposite Chainpur. The river Sanjay was then in flood and rebels found the Thakur of Kharsawan on the opposite bank with two guns and a large number of men to oppose their landing. But at this point messengers came from the Raja, escorted the mutineers to Chakradharpur where they were fed and allowed to keep guard over their arms.[14] The Thakur of Kharsawan played the role of a detached spectator. There is no evidence to show that he either pursued or interfered with the rebels, may be due to fear, may be due to his motive of watching the trend of events for taking a final prudent step.

After the departure of Major Sissmore the government appointed Lieutenant Birch as the Assistant Commissioner of the district with a definite order to reoccupy Chaibasa.[15] Even in the midst of conflicting opinions regarding the exact date of rising of the sepoys at Chaibasa one fact is at least certain that on and from 5 August 1857 right up to the reoccupation of Chaibasa on 16 September 1857 there was practically no British rule. The Raja of Seraikella to whom the authority of administering the district was entrusted by Major Sissmore had faded out from the picture. The reoccupation of Chaibasa was essential for maintaining British prestige. When Lt. Birch arrived at Seraikella on 13 September[16] he found the chief along with his associate the Thakur of Kharsawan ready to help him. Preparations were briskly made from 13 September 1857. Lt. Birch reoccupied Chaibasa on 16 September 1857 with the help of the faithful Raja of Seraikella, the zamindar of Kharsawan and 3000 Kols.[17] On 19 September 1857, Birch requested Arjun Singh to come to Chaibasa and help him in strengthening British position. The request was treated with contempt. Birch also sent messengers throughout Kolhan to judge the views of the people of the district. They informed him that tribals of the places adjacent to Porahat refused to meet him as they were going in large numbers either to Chakradharpur or Ajodhya, a *lakhiraj* village belonging to Porahat Raja. He further learnt from a Ho *dafadar* of his court, who had been deputed to ascertain what was going on, that Arjun Singh was planning an attack on Seraikella and the tribesmen were obeying his summons for this purpose. Jagu Dewan, a man in the employ of the Raja, was making preparations to establish a military post at Ajodhya.[18] On 21 September Dubro Manki brought an arrow to Birch which had been for a short time in circulation. Most probably it came from the members of the tribe inhabiting the territories of Porahat Raja.[19] The deposition of Dubro Manki recorded by Birch on 10 October 1857 runs thus :

> 'Mosa Mankee gave me the arrow, and desired me to pass it on to Pookria, Ussoora and so on to Ponda Mankee and Bukelya Manki's illaqua ; and to pass this word with it that all the Mankees were to assemble their people armed, at Rajah Urjoon Singh's place at Chuckerdurpore; the Rajah is going to fight the Seraikeylah Rajah.'[20]

The circulation of the arrow amongst the Hos was the signal for taking up arms. So it served as an alarm to the British administrator at Chaibasa. Birch sent a *parwanh* 'commanding the Raja for having secured the mutineers and calling upon him to give them up to him at Vasahatu.' This was also turned down. Birch thereupon sent Babu Ram Prasad Singh, uncle of the Thakur of Kharsawan, Narayan Mukhtar of the Keonjhar Raja and Babu Raghubar Singh of Icha, a friend of the Porahat Raja, to solicit his co-operation and assistance. But these moves were utterly ineffective.[21] In spite of the fact that he was armed with 3000 Hos and getting co-operation from Seraikella and Kharsawan, besides the British army under his command, Birch could not resort to action. This goes to show the strength of the preparation on the part of Raja Arjun Singh. The reason for all these commands, requests and persuasions for the Raja's co-operation was that the whole atmosphere of Chotanagpur was saturated with the spirit of revolt. The Raja too was active all the while. While on the one hand to placate the British he professed his loyalty to them[22] on the other to strengthen his own position further he began to negotiate for help from outside. He posted a contingent at Ajodhya, an important outpost of his territory, under the charge of Jagu Dewan. Jagu wrote a letter on 27 September 1857 to a shopkeeper at Chaibasa 'calling upon him to provide rations for 10,000 men.'[23]

The preparations on the side of the ruler of Porahat unnerved the British. Birch declared him to be a rebel, confiscated his estates, and offered Rs. 1000 as reward for his person.[24] Even then Arjun Singh informed Birch of his intentions to deliver the treasure and rebels to him at Chaibasa. But he soon changed his mind and instead proceeded to Ranchi. The road to Ranchi from Chakradharpur in those days was a circuitous and difficult one covering a distance of more than 70 miles. It was also contiguous to the territories of the Thakur of Kera, a staunch adherent of the British, who could at any time intervene to protect the interest of the allies. But such was the popularity of the Raja that he was confident that he could easily overcome any obstacle. At Ranchi Arjun Singh delivered the treasure and the sepoys to Captain Davis [25] and solemnly promised to meet Birch immediately after his return to Chakradharpur. According to Halliday the soldiers so delivered were 100 and they 'were sentenced, 43 to be hung, and the remainder to transportation or imprisonment for various terms. The sentences were carried out.'[26]

In spite of all the support Arjun Singh got on and from 5 August 1857, the action taken by him in surrendering the sepoys, who had reposed so much confidence in him, seems really mysterious. Was he still hesitating to wage war against the British or did he mean by all these preparations an attack on Seraikella? He was prone to believe one of the rebel proclamations that British rule in India had come to an end. But he was not to be led away by this alone. He knew very well that one false step would ruin the very cause for which he was fighting. He was very cautious in his move and before actually plunging head long in any war he wanted to ensure that his men remained faithful to the cause and to him and not to side with the government or the Raja of Seraikella. He had planned to launch an attack on Seraikella and with this aim in view had actually established a military post at Ajodhya on the road from Chakradharpur to Seraikella. In spite of all his preparations, however, he did not deem it wise to attack Seraikella at that time being aware of the fact that the British authority at Chaibasa was solely under the influence of its chief. But in case the British were forced to leave India the inevitable result would be a war for supremacy in the district between him and his enemy, the ruler of Seraikella.

Up to the time of his surrendering the sepoys and the treasure Arjun Singh had not done anything which might have amounted to waging war against the British. Captain Dalton remarked that Arjun Singh 'had not even contemplated treason, and was at heart no ill-wisher to the British Government.'[27] If it was actually so why after all he changed his mind? One reason was perhaps that when he expected to be received with commendation at Ranchi Arjun Singh was treated with utmost coldness and suspicion. But this was not all. The government meant further humiliation to him peremptorily requiring him to immediately proceed to Chaibasa and to 'present himself humbly and submissively to Lieutenant Birch on pain of being dealt with as a rebel.' In case of disobedience he was threatened with imprisonment.[28]

Arjun Singh was allowed, however, to proceed to Chakradharpur and from there to report himself at once to Birch. He returned to Chakradharpur, a sadder and perhaps a wiser man, sadder because so many brave souls were sacrificed and wiser because he could now read the intention of the government better. At Chakradharpur, he found his palace under the control of the Sub-Assistant Commissioner, acting under the orders of Birch. The cup of misery was full, the climax of indignity and insult was reached, and like a wounded lion the Raja retired to Porahat with his family. To quote Captain Dalton: 'Driven from his house and his property seized he and his followers appear to have flung themselves headlong into revolt.'[29]

It may be mentioned here that when the Raja retired to Porahat with his family there was not even an attempt at resistance. Even then the situation was so tense that out of fear the Sub-Assistant Commissioner 'precipitately abandoned' his charge. Jagu took advantage of the situation to reoccupy Chakradharpur.[30] Birch thought of making an attempt of subjugating Chakradharpur, being reinforced by 100 Sikhs under Captain Montgomery.[31] Accordingly on 21 November 1857 accompanied by Captain Hale and a detachment of Sikhs, Birch took possession of Porahat. But the Raja escaped and was not, for some time, heard of.[32] About the attack of Chakradharpur Col. Malleson, however, gives us an entirely different picture of the events. He says 'Hale supported by the followers of one of the local chieftains (meaning thereby the chief of Seraikella), attacked and dispersed the followers of pretender. But for some time the insurrection remained unsubdued.'[33]

From these conflicting reports we can correctly deduce that it was not the Raja who was then pursued for he was then at Porahat, a score of miles away from Chakradharpur, actual scene of occurrence. The above version regarding the occupation of Porahat and the escape of the Raja seem exaggerations when compared with the following lines from Halliday's Minute of 30 September 1858. This also apprised us with the activities of Arjun Singh and Jagu Dewan. To quote:

> 'He (Arjun Singh) was said to be completely in the hands of his dewan, a man named Juggo, for whose apprehension,...a reward had been before offered by the Government. This man was reported to be doing his best to excite the Kols to rise, and using all his influence with the Raja to prevent his submitting himself to Lieutenant Birch.
>
> The Raja, however, still continued to profess his loyalty and his intention of keeping his pledges,... Lieutenant Birch, (who had, in the meantime, been reinforced by 100 Sikhs under Captain Montgomery), for some time took no active steps against the Raja,...as having proved his sincerity by giving up the mutineers and treasure.'[34]

This goes to prove that Jagu Dewan was the person who was then deemed more dangerous by the British for his supposed complete influence over the Raja. More so perhaps for his ability to rouse such sentiments amongst the Hos as would turn their minds against the foreigners. So at that point of time the Raja was not their main target whom the British still considered to be loyal to them. Naturally the wrath of the British fell on this obstacle in the path of their maintaining hold over their newly acquired territories in Singhbhum.

Towards the end of November Jagu was captured in a surprise attack. He was summarily tried, sentenced and hanged.[35] There is, however, some difference of opinion regarding the date of the sad end of this brave Dewan. According to Dalton this was on 20 October 1857.[36] Lushington recorded the date of the attack by Birch as 21 November 1857.[37] So, if not exactly on 21 November 1857 the sad 'execution' must have taken place a day or two later.

Jagu Dewan, 'a young man scarcely above 20 years of age',[38] was a man of great potentiality and of grim determination. It was but natural that the British should dub him as 'a man of well known bad character'[39] and offer a reward for his capture. Jagu had made it the mission of his life to carry on infinite propaganda against the aliens and to rouse the sons of the soil against them. It was through his efforts that the Hoṣ in Kolhan 'were solemnly sworn to obey no orders, but those of Urjoon Singh.'[40] The British, therefore, felt that Jagu was their archenemy and the sooner they got rid of him the better it was for their interest. The day after Jagu was caught and hanged the British force attempted to surprise the Raja at Porahat. The Raja's house at Porahat was attacked, gutted and destroyed, eighty of his villages reduced to ashes and one thousand head of cattle were carried off by Birch.[41] Again the Chief of Seraikella afforded great assistance to Birch, as did the local zamindars and petty chiefs, all of whom were suitably rewarded for the services rendered.[42]

The above acts of the British were sufficient provocations for throwing off all semblance of the slightest feeling of tolerance towards the British that might have lingered in the mind of the Raja. The letter that he wrote about this time to his brother Baijnath Singh[43] informed that he was collecting forces; and that it was his desire that his brother should fight and never allow the enemy to escape.

Porahat and its adjoining areas began their efforts for giving the foreigners a square fight. Those who could serve as soldiers voluntarily offered their services; those who had money volunteered to pay double the rents to enable the Raja to mobilise his forces and blacksmiths were active in moulding and casting matchlocks and iron-balls in anticipation of the ensuing battle. From Dalton we learn that twelve blacksmiths were engaged in making iron balls for Raja's ordnance.[44] Thus a serious anti-British atmosphere had been created. Even the British had to report about 'the existence of widespread insurrection amongst the various tribes in Singhbhum'.[45]

Arjun Singh then contemplated systematic military operations to execute his plans of retaliation successfully. Thakur of Kera, a relative of Raja Arjun Singh who had joined Birch against him, was the first target of attack. His house and the adjoining bazar were attacked, plundered and burnt by an army of 2000 men under Baijnath Singh and Raghu Deo on 24 December 1857.[46] The British managed with great difficulty to disperse the enemy but dared not continue the pursuit. Baijnath Singh and Raghu Deo then led the insurgents towards Ajodhya on the Chakradharpur-Seraikella road. At Ajodhya about 2000 insurgents assembled and planned an attack on Chaibasa.[47] Simultaneously with this southern Kolhan too was in arms against the British. The British naturally became concerned about the security of Chaibasa.[48] The military cunning of the Raja in keeping the enemy engaged on several fronts and mobilizing all possible forces was successful in unnerving the British who had to suffer several reverses, and were for the time being paralysed. Even Dalton had to admit that 'Nothing more could be done till reinforcement arrived.'[49]

It was about this time that the murder of Jaintgarh police by the rebels took place. This was treated as a definite signal for an outbreak in southern Kolhan.[50] The Hos of southern Kolhan, tenacious, bold and warlike, had in the past always maintained a laudable standard of anti-Britishism. To recapitulate, these brave people of the south incited their softer brethren of the northern Kolhan to a rebellion in 1821. It was natural that the community more or less ruminated the bright days of the past when they were independent. They could not forget the events which led to their subjugation by the British who had promised to maintain them and their tribal traditions according to the terms agreed upon in 1821. How could they forget the glorious happenings during the 'Kol Rebellion' of

1831 when the warlike Hos had completely routed a British army in the field at Jikilata. While British rule was abominable to them they at the same time looked with suspicion upon all the ruling chiefs of the district. But for Arjun Singh they had nothing but love and complete confidence. Even Lieutenant-Governor Halliday had to admit: 'his influence amongst the Kols was great.'[51] Captain Dalton similarly observed: 'His great influence over the Coles by whom he is regarded with the reverence due to the Deity.'[52] Under the leadership of Arjun Singh the anti-British uprising engulfed almost the entire district.

The insurgents carried on simultaneous and successful attacks in Kolhan and Porahat.[53] This insurgency was an open challenge to the mighty Imperium. On 25 December 1857 Captain Hale's party, supported by the followers of the Seraikella Raja, attacked and dispersed a large assemblage of the Hos and others led by Baijnath Singh. But as the rebellion could not be effectually quelled, the Shekawati battalion under Colonel Foster, (mentioned in some dispatches and letters as Colonel Forster), who was at this time at Raniganj, was directed to move to Chaibasa at the earliest.[54]

Meanwhile the Raja and his brother Baijnath Singh were trying to organise a more formidable opposition against the British. There was an insurrection in Bor *pir* in south Kolhan under the leadership of village headmen of that *pir*. One jamadar and two *barkandazes* were killed. When the British authorities at Chaibasa were informed of this happening they decided to march against the insurgents. On 14 January 1858 Lushington, the Officiating Commissioner of Manbhum and Singhbhum, along with the Senior Assistant Commissioner Lieutenant Birch and a regiment of 50 or 60 Sikhs under captain Hale marched towards Bor *pir*. They succeeded only in capturing two of the petty 'Sardars' (headmen). But as they were preparing to return to the station a small body of insurgents opposed them on the bank of the river Mogra. The British army under Captain Hale could disperse them easily, and having destroyed a village which they had reached, evidently to scare away the rebels, marched on a different route. When the army had just crossed the deep bed of a dry *nala* they were surprised by 3000 or 4000 insurgents who from their jungle hideouts came into the open showering the enemies with arrows. Not an officer escaped unhurt. Captain Hale, commanding the Sikhs, was wounded in 4 places; Lt. Birch's arm was pinned to his side by an arrow, while, Lushington and Dr. Hayes, the only other officials present, were also, though less severely, wounded. Of the 50 Sikhs, 25 were more or less severely wounded, one of whom mortally, and one man was killed. The casualty among the insurgents was stated to be 150. But the fierceness of attack so unnerved the English arms that they decided at once to return to Chaibasa leaving their 'tent equipage' behind, lest the enemy should cut off the retreat, thus making it almost impossible to force their way to the station. The insurgent Hos however made an unrelented pursuit for a distance of 7 miles. But they were kept in check by the steady retaliation of unwounded men, who protected the rear, and the station was reached without further casualty.[55]

From the above account of the encounter at Mogra given by no less a personality than the Lieutenant-Governor of Bengal himself it is proved beyond doubt that the British army had been worsted. The claim of one dead, as a price of retreat, seems preposterous. Courtesy Malleson we learn about 'the large casualty roll'.[56] The net result of the reverses at Mogra had been disheartening for the 'loyal servants' of the British.[57] But this was indeed a proud achievement which encouraged the brave insurgents to carry on their fight for freedom.

The rebels then made an attack on Chakradharpur, residence of the Raja of Porahat which was then occupied by the Raja of Seraikella. The defeat of the British forces, under officers on whom the Company government had great reliance, was definitely discouraging to the ruler of Seraikella who thought it wiser to substitute discretion for valour. An attack by the section of the forces of liberation was sufficient to infuse terror in his heart and in spite of being armed with 300 matchlocks, two guns and a host of soldiers he preferred to leave Chakradharpur.[58]

The situation was too humiliating for the British to stand. So Colonel Foster had to be requisitioned for bringing the situation under control. Foster reached Chaibasa having made rapid marches by 17 January 1858 with his Shekawati Battalion. Chakradharpur was made the first target of his attack for reasons more than one. The civil population there had witnessed that the Raja of Seraikella in spite of being fully armed had surrendered and fled and the rebels had gained in prestige. Moreover, the people there might have been feeling all the time that anti-British revolt was bound to succeed.

The insurgents did not like to face Col. Foster who was fully armed. Though there was no actual fight Foster carried on pillage and plunder and looted a large quantity of grain and cattle. He then reconquered Chakradharpur.[59] But that was not everything he was called upon to do. The British prestige in southern Kolhan was yet to be restored. This was not an easy task and so before launching the campaign in Kolhan it was necessary to seek reinforcement.

When the reinforcement of 50 European sailors arrived from Midnapur Col. Foster began his march towards south Kolhan. He had not to proceed very long in his journey to meet with the first and one of the most formidable oppositions at Serengsia,[60] a hill pass not more than 15 miles from Chaibasa. Here were hidden well-armed Hos ready to shoot at the enemy on its way to south Kolhan. The tactics adopted spoke well of the military planning of these fighters numbering about ten thousand men armed with bows and arrows under Raghu Deo.[61] They allowed the enemy to cross the hill-pass and when they were descending the southern side of the hill the insurgents showered volleys of arrows. The British army under Col. Foster was taken by surprise. According to a tradition of the locality the losses they suffered were many. The Hos scarcely maintained any records of their activities but memories of the glorious actions at Serengsia like the achievements at Jikilata have been treasured in community memory, being handed down from father to son. Though Halliday in his Minute remarked: 'It is unnecessary to give the details of the different expeditions,'[62] we learn from a British source that only Captain of the company of Sikh troops survived and he too had to cover a distance of 30 miles to reach Chaibasa to save his life.[63] After this the Hos sought shelter in the jungles with only a few losses. Even after this reverse a cruel invader like Col. Foster, who earned the notoriety of committing so many acts of arson, pillage and plunder in the villages near Chakradharpur, could not even think of pursuing the enemy. This had an adverse effect on the British army. On the other hand, the Hos were now convinced that they were not unequal rivals of the British though the latter had the advantages of being equipped with such arms and ammunitions compared to which the bow and the arrow or the battle-axe were most primitive.

In the meantime Arjun Singh had planned to mobilise rebel sepoys from other places. They had been directed to assemble at Chakradharpur. But while they were crossing the *ghats* the Raja of Seraikella and the Thakur of Kera intercepted them. The Raja thereupon wrote a letter to Biswanath Sahi Deo of Barkagarh on the Falgun 1265, corresponding with 15 February 1858, stating that he (the Raja) was in the hills with 8,400 men and was fighting with the sahibs. He requested him to send arms and ammunitions and declared his intention of burning Chaibasa. All the reverses of the British army in the hands of the rebels had meanwhile sapped their morale as evidenced by the proposals for conciliation they sent to the Raja. One such was made by Mewa Lall, an employee of the Company government, in his letter written to Baijnath Singh on 17 March 1858. He requested him to dismiss the insurgents collected by him, to release the Keonjhar Baboos and others who were made captives and to lay down arms to the British. Another instance was Assistant Commissioner Captain Moncrieff's letter to Baijnath Singh on 20 March 1858 requesting him to decide whether he would fight with the government or come to their side. But all these persuasions were of no consequence. The rebels were determined to make attacks on Chaibasa, Chakradharpur and Kera. With this aim in view they mustered strong and on 26 March 1858 encircled the camp of Moncrieff. The resolute and desperate body of 2000 armed Hos, could with great difficulty, be dispersed but not beaten.[64] In April 1858 the rebel army decided to recapture Chakradharp which had temporarily been occupied by Col. Foster. F

Captain Dalton's letter of 30 September 1859 we find that at this time the rebel army made Jumroo, a place four miles west of Chakradharpur, their base. The leader of the rebel army was Baijnath Singh and his lieutenants were Raghu Deo, Sham Karan and others.

Chakradharpur was surrounded and attacked by a vast ring of armed Hos. They killed six Europeans and burnt six villages in Kera. The British claimed to have repulsed the attack and driven the rebels from Jumroo without suffering any casualty.[65] In spite of this claim we find that efforts were made by the British to win over the Raja to their side. On 19 April 1858 Moncrieff once again requested the Raja to come to terms and Mewa Lall also made a similar request on the same day. Arjun Singh did not care about such overtures and carried on his programme of war. Being exasperated and convinced of the fact that the Raja was indomitable the British forces under Weldon, First officer of the Naval Brigade, accompanied by Scott and Seraikella forces as usual, attacked the camps of the insurgents. The British army started indulging in their usual plunder and pillage and were marching on when unexpectedly they found themselves 'surrounded by the enemy who from the height poured down a shower of arrows and matchlock balls.'[66]

The official version is silent about what had happened on this occasion. There is not even the common and usual record of heavy casualties on the side of the rebel army and none of the British forces. What had actually happened was that they had to make a retreat. One can safely draw this conclusion from a proclamation by the Commissioner dated 26 May 1858.[67] This called upon all the raiyats and others in Kolhan and Porahat to submit quietly, and to resume cultivation. It assured that if there be any trouble or poverty, arrangements would be made to protect them from starvation; pardon would be extended to all, except those who had been proclaimed by name or would be found guilty or having been principals in or accessory to cold-blooded atrocious murders. From the tone of this proclamation one can very reasonably deduce that the wave of insurrection in the district of

Singhbhum was definitely alarming to the British whose attempts to stop these risings had proved abortive. This is amply borne out by the fact that even after the claim of successfully repulsing enemy attack Dalton had to admit that the country continued in a very disturbed state.[68] That is why such requests were repeated from time to time by the British authority in the district of Singhbhum and scornfully rejected by the Raja. The lasting effect of so many atrocities on poor and innocent people was so bitter in the minds of the Raja and his men that they could no longer be persuaded to yield to any terms offered by the British. Captain Dalton, the Commissioner and the Agent to the Governor-General-in-Council, came to Chaibasa to watch the reaction of the proclamation on the minds of those for whom it was meant. Finding that the proclamation did not evoke any response he issued a *parwana* on 2 June 1858, impressing upon Arjun Singh to come and see him. During this period, the insurgents met with success in every instance and the position of the British was thoroughly jeopardized and their prestige on the wane. Arjun Singh proudly refused to comply.

On 9 June 1858 some thousands of Hos composing the rebel army under Raghu Deo surrounded the camp of the Naval Brigade at Chakradharpur and Captain Moncrieff. The latter was returning from Chaibasa, where he had been to see the Commissioner. But the enemy attack forced him to withdraw to the camp. Attacks were repeated on 10 and 11 June. Apprehending that he might have to face more assault, Weldon, First Officer of the Naval Brigade stationed at Chakradharpur, before launching any campaign, thought of reinforcing himself. He was actually reinforced by an army under Lieutenant Reeves. Yet no counter attack was made by the British. Halliday in his dispatch to the Governor-General of India, however, claimed that 'A pursuit was attempted, but was soon abandoned on account of the extreme heat.'[69]

The reason for abandoning the pursuit, as stated by the Lieutenant-Governor, does not however appear to be convincing. The fact appears to be that reverses that the British army had suffered so many times during the year were sufficient grounds for desisting from a pursuit. The British claimed to have driven the rebels to the hills and kept the area free from any disturbance till November. But it was also a tall claim. Though insurgents avoided attacking the British posts, they freely indulged in making night forages into unprotected villages and in loot and arson. The situation reached its peak in November when Anandpur was attacked by a force under Baijnath Singh and Raghu Deo. The Thakur of Anandpur had all along inclinations to submit to the British. Naturally the rebels considered him an archenemy. The British were bound by their pledge to support him in case of an attack on his territory by the insurgent army. There is nothing to show that on this occasion the British army dared extend their helping hands towards the defence of Anandpur. This virtually gave the rebel army free hand to attack Anandpur and drive the Thakur away.[70] The success of the insurgents on this and other different occasions definitely speaks of the incapacity of the British in repressing them.

From July 1858 onwards the British army could do nothing to arrest the activities of Arjun Singh. From the abstract translation of letters written on *tal*-leaves we find that after July 1858 the people of Saranda *pir* were brought under the banner of Arjun Singh; measures were taken by the rebel forces to surround the British army at Aijhurrun *ghat* in case Lieutenant Birch attacked Anandpur territory; other *ghats* in the district were guarded; fresh forces were recruited and Arjun Singh actually contemplated the establishment of a *thana* at Karaikela with a view to cut off all communications and supplies from Ranchi. Arjun Singh wrote to Baijnath Singh on 14 November 1858 stating that some Hos had joined him, that Lt. Birch ("the Sahib") had received a *perwana* which he was not to open till he had collected the zamindars, that Birch had a very small force and was not then preparing any expedition.[71] The situation was such that Captain Dalton had to make an earnest request for immediate reinforcement to the Naval Brigade in the district.[72]

Arjun Singh was practically uncontrollable. In strategy and military operations he was perhaps inferior to none. It was found that during all these months he could consolidate his position and gather fresh support. The British had then no other way but to take recourse to the mediation by the Raja of Mayurbhanj, father-in-law of the Raja of Porahat.[73] The Raja of Mayurbhanj sent messengers to his son-in-law, advising him to come to terms with the British. But from abstract translation of letters written on *tal*-leaves by Arjun Singh to Baijnath Singh on 13 January 1859 we learn that he had already written to the Mayurbhanj Raja conveying that he would respect any advice he received except advice to surrender.[74] To the British the Raja however gave an 'evasive and unsatisfactory reply' to the proposal for amnesty and it gave the government 'no expectation of his surrender.'[75] On the contrary reports were received that on 14 January 1859 Arjun Singh had issued proclamation to the raiyats of Anandpur assuring them that he had taken them under his special protection.[76] Reports were received that south Kolhan was again astir and attack on the *thana* at Jaintgarh was apprehended. Accordingly *pykes* furnished from Keonjhar were posted at the *thana* for protection.[77]

The British force stationed in Singhbhum was palpably inadequate to counter this situation. So Dalton was compelled to frantically request the government for military help.[78] Far from adopting offensive military operations against the Raja the immediate problem that baffled the British authorities was the establishment of a post where they could maintain themselves until the arrival of reinforcement as prayed for. Captain Dalton wrote: 'It was, therefore, considered advisable both by Lieutenant Birch and myself that he should proceed from Dulyekellah (Dalaikela) with a force into Bur Peer and occupy himself in quieting it till we were in a position to resume offensive operations.'[79] Birch proceeded with a force consisting of 15 men of the Naval Brigade under Williams and one 12 pounder Howitzer, 100 Ho and Santal levy, the whole under Lieutenant Reeves. But he found the road blockaded. Not only this the insurgents occupied a small *ghat* on the road between Asantalia and Chakradharpur with a view to intercept all communications and supplies between these two posts.[80] In this attempt they succeeded. The idea behind the blockade was that while Birch would continue his march from Dalaikela to

Bor *pir* fully convinced about regular supply of ammunition, ration and advice he would ultimately, find to his utter dismay that he was forlorn. This bespeaks of the military genius of the Raja. The forces of liberation conducted their offensive operations from the thickly forested hills and inflicted casualties on the enemy with minimum loss on their side. It was this suddenness which the British could not anticipate.

Lt. Yates was sent to make the *ghat* free but he failed to do so. Accordingly a contingent led by Green of Indian Navy pushed on to Dalaikela and arrived safe at that post but not without some 'trifling' opposition.[81] Trifling though it might have been termed by Captain Dalton the facts were otherwise. The rebels were determined to frustrate the attempts of the British army in their onward march for the occupation of some footholds in Bor *pir*. The insurrection throughout the district was well planned and the mustering of the rebels at Anandpur and Saranda further strengthened them. This drove Captain Dalton almost to the verge of despair and he earnestly sought for the co-operation of Col. Foster.[82] It is indeed strange that, even though Captain Dalton was getting constant military help from the British authorities as well from the chiefs of Mayurbhanj, Keonjhar, Sambalpur, Seraikella and Kharsawan and the Thakurs of Kera and Anandpur, he should have implored for further reinforcement.

Meanwhile Lt. Birch who could arrive at Bor *pir* to quieten the tense situation prevailing there began his fresh march from Kotegarh via Jamda towards Saranda. The plan of the rebels was to attack Birch from the rear while he was on his march to Saranda. But unfortunately Birch was apprised of the intended attack and was on his guard before he proceeded. However, Raghu Deo, the leader of the opposite camp, was too clever to be caught napping. The result was that there was no encounter although, as reported by Birch himself, the rebels were able to create panic among the *pykes* from Keonjhar and Seraikella so much so that Birch had to wait and request for reinforcement. On the arrival of an additional contingent, however, the march was resumed.[83]

The wilds of Saranda *pir*, inaccessible in many places even now, were an unknown tract to the foreigners. It was in these thickly forested areas that the British troops would contact a clan which was, for some reason or other, opposed to the Raja. The leader of this clan was one Boodhoo Toon who offered the British forces every possible succor and promised to guide them to a place where the Raja was contemplating ambuscade. It was on this hazardous march through hills and dales that Birch was assured of the advances of the people of Anandpur to join him. He observed—'I am happy also to be able to report that the people of Anandpur are readily joining us, and that Babu Chakradhar Singh, the uncle of the young Thakur, is exerting himself to the utmost to furnish supplies and procure information.'[84]

The Raja of Porahat was nevertheless alert all along and he had every information regarding the intended expedition. His men accordingly blockaded the narrow hill-pass at Amjora.[85] So Birch had to encounter the toughest resistance. The events thereafter are still veiled with mystery as the information from the British did scarcely fit in with the elaborate military situation of both the sides. We learn that 'Lt. Birch, on the 29th ultimo (January 1859)...after a long and difficult forced march from Deepa surprised the adherents of the Ex-Rajah of Porahat.'[86] From the scanty evidence available so far in the shape of a letter from Captain Dalton to A.R. Young, Secretary to the Government of Bengal written on 21 February 1859 from Camp Chaibasa, the military position of the Raja might be somewhat assessed. The letter was mainly based on the report of Birch to Captain Dalton. As any information from the other side is unavailable, we have to depend on the one-sided version of the British administrator who like Dupleix rejoiced in making mention of their own success, while never caring to allude to any repulses. We can surmise that they had to face resistance from the opposite side, particularly when they had to deal with a formidable opponent like the Raja who had kept them engaged, seldom giving them rest for a period of about a year and a half. The letter refers to the capture or unconditional surrender of nearly all the Porahat insurgents including the Raja who surrendered on the morning of 16 February 1859, while his brother Baijnath Singh had surrendered earlier, *i.e.* on 10 February 1859.[87] To achieve this the whole force of the district including the contingents supplied by the rulers of Keonjhar, Seraikella and Kharsawan were employed. Moreover the British army was positively helped by the secret information that the Raja was at Dhipa (described by Captain Dalton as Deepa) in Saranda hill section.[88]

However, the above information has to be accepted with a grain of salt. If there were elaborate military preparations on the British side the concentration of forces by the Raja was of no mean magnitude. If an elaborate system of espionage so common with the British in those days was at work against the Raja there is no reason to believe that the Raja would remain uninformed of the strategies of his enemy. Had it not been so he could not have kept the British engaged almost to their wit's end for such a long time;[89] had it not been so he could not have forced them to implore the assistance of the Raja of Mayurbhanj as their mediator. One would not naturally be inclined to believe that after being compelled to take recourse to all the assistance available from the neighbouring chieftains and being dragged to the dire necessity of requisitioning an additional force of nearly 100 men of the Naval Brigade the capture of the insurgents, the adherents of the Raja and the ultimate surrender of Arjun Singh could be effected without a major clash about which there is no mention in all these letters.

The design of deliberately desisting from making any mention of the happenings between 29 January 1859 and 15 February 1859 is significant. The fact nevertheless remains that the Raja had ultimately to surrender because the combined forces of the British and the local chiefs were stronger than that of his own and of the intervention, with ample assurances by his father-in-law, the Raja of Mayurbhanj[90] that his interests might be duly looked after. Not only this the shape of events in the neighbouring districts and the country as a whole had so changed that the fond hope of receiving aid from outside could no longer be cherished. The barren tract of land that was Singhbhum could no longer sustain any large congregation of men in the shape of an army. Even those who were inspired with the noble ideas of liberating their country from foreign domination could not possibly continue an unequal fight of the bow and the arrow any longer, or a few matchlocks against the rifle and the canon. So the inevitable happened. With the surrender of the Raja the popular uprising came to an end. Captain Dalton remarked: 'Those who had been in arms returned to their houses and ordinary pursuits like lambs to a fold.'[91]

Thus the mighty British Raj finally put out the embers of the popular revolt. Nevertheless, the saga of bravery and indomitable courage of a people and their leader to protect their freedom left an indelible impression on the course of history adding a glorious chapter to India's struggle for freedom.

NOTES AND REFERENCES

1. C.E. Buckland, *Bengal under the Lieutenant Governors*, Vol. 1, Calcutta, 1901, p. 98.
2. G.B. Malleson, *History of the Indian Mutiny 1857-58*, Vol. IV, p. 95.
3. Buckland, *Bengal*, p. 99.
4. *Ibid.*
5. E.T. Dalton to E.H. Lushington, 30 September 1859. Spare Copies of Porahat Papers from 1857 to 1862. (SCPP), BSA.
6. E.H. Lushington, the Officiating Commissioner of Manbhum and Singhbhum to the Secretary to the Government of Bengal, 29 December 1857, para 3 (SCPP, BSA).
7. Lushington to the Secretary, 29 December 1857, para 4.
8. Malleson, *History*, p. 96.
9. W. Grey, Secretary to the Government of India, Home Department, to W.S. Seton Karr, Secretary to the Government of Bengal, 18 April 1861, para 8 (SCPP, BSA).
10. Lushington to the Secretary, 29 December 1857, para 4.
11. R.C. Birch to the Secretary to the Government of Bengal 6 October 1857, para 4 (SCPP, BSA); Lushington to the Secretary, para 9.
12. Lushington to the Secretary, 29 December 1857, para 5.
13. *Ibid.*, para 6.
14. *Ibid.*, para 7.
15. Grey to Seton Karr, 18 April 1861, para 8.
16. Lushington to the Secretary, 29 December 1857, para 10.
17. Buckland, *Bengal*, p. 103.
18. Birch to the Secretary, 6 October 1857, paras 6-7.
19. *Ibid.*, para 7.
20. Dalton to Lushington, 30 September 1859.

21. Lushington to the Secretary, 29 December 1857, para 11.
22. *Ibid.*, paras 13-14.
23. *Ibid.*, para 16.
24. *Ibid.*, para 17.
25. Grey to Seton Karr, 18 April 1861, paras 11-12.
26. Buckland, *Bengal*, p. 105, E.T. Dalton to A.R. Young, the Secretary to the Government of Bengal, 10 May 1858, para 2 (SCPP, BSA).
27. Dalton to Lusington, 30 September 1859, para 32.
28. Letter of the Secretary to the Government of Bengal to the Officiating Commissioner of Chotanagpur, 15 October 1857 (SCPP, BSA).
29. Dalton to Lushington, 30 September 1859, para 32.
30. Grey to Seton Karr, 18 April 1861, para 14.
31. Buckland, *Bengal*, p. 105.
32. Lushington to the Secretary, 29 December 1857, para 22.
33. Malleson, *History*, p. 306.
34. Buckland, *Bengal*, p. 105.
35. *Ibid.*
36. Dalton to Lushington, 30 September 1859, para 30.
37. Lushington to the Secretary, 29 December 1857, para 22.
38. Birch to the Secretary, 6 October 1857, para 16.
39. Lushington to the Secretary, 29 December 1857, para 16.
40. Birch to the Secretary, 6 October 1857, para 9.
41. Dalton to Lushington, 30 September 1859, para 30.
42. Buckland, *Bengal*, p. 105.
43. Dalton to Lushington, 30 September 1859, Appendix A.
44. *Ibid.*, para 31.
45. Buckland, *Bengal*, p. 106.
46. Dalton to Lushington, 30 September 1859, para 7.
47. *Ibid.*
48. *Ibid.*, para 34.
49. *Ibid.*
50. *Ibid.*, para 33.
51. Buckland, *Bengal*, p. 105.
52. Dalton to Sir John Peter Grant, Lt. Governor of Bengal, 26 June 1861 (SCPP, BSA).
53. Lushington to the Secretary, 29 December 1857.
54. Buckland, *Bengal*, p. 106.
55. *Ibid.*, pp. 106-7.
56. Malleson, *History*, Vol. IV, p. 306.
57. O'Malley, *Bengal District Gazetteer*, p. 40.
58. Buckland, *Bengal*, p. 107.
59. *Ibid.*; Dalton to Lushington, 30 September 1859, para 34.
60. Buckland, *Bengal*, p. 107.
61. F.B. Bradley Birt, *Chota Nagpore: A Litle known Province of the Empire*, London, 1903, p. 226.

62. Buckland, *Bengal*, p. 107. This comment would not have been evoked had there been anything to record regarding the valour of the British army. The Minute however did not leave out details regarding the commencement of submission of some elements which evidently was more the result of the unusual diplomatic tactics of the British than of their prowess in battlefields.
63. *Ibid.*
64. Dalton to Lushington, 30 September 1859, para 34.
65. *Ibid.*, para
66. Buckland, *Bengal*, p. 109.
67. Dalton to Lushington, 30 September 1859, Appendix B.
68. *Ibid.*
69. Buckland, *Bengal*, p. 109. It is interesting to note that Dalton merely mentions "another attack was made on the 10th June 1858 by a force under Ruggo Deo" without providing any details. Dalton to Lushington, 30 September 1859, para 34. This proves that the information provided by the British do not contain the whole truth.
70. Dalton to Lushington, 30 September 1859, para 36.
71. *Ibid.*, Appendix.
72. Dalton to the Secretary to the Government of Bengal, 8 November 1858.
73. Dalton to Young, 1 January 1859, para 3 (SCPP, BSA).
74. Dalton to Lushington, 30 September 1859, Appendix A.
75. Dalton to A.R. Young, 1 January 1859, para 1.
76. Dalton to Lushington, 30 September 1859, Appendix A.
77. Dalton to A.R. Young, 1 January 1859, para 4.
78. *Ibid.*, para 5.
79. *Ibid.*
80. *Ibid.*
81. *Ibid.*, para 6.
82. *Ibid.*
83. Lt. Birch, Senior Assistant Commissioner, Singhbhum Division, to the Commissioner of Chotanagpur, 26 January 1859, para 3 (SCPP, BSA).
84. *Ibid.*, para 8.
85. *Ibid.*, para 9.
86. Dalton to Young, 1 February 1859, para 1 (SCPP, BSA).
87. Dalton to Young, 21 February 1859 (SCPP, BSA).
88. Dalton to Young, 1 February 1859, para 1.
89. The statement of W. Grey supports this. He observed 'After remaining in rebellion to upwards of a year, during which he gave a good deal of trouble to our troops.' W. Grey to W.S. Seton Karr, 18 April 1861, para 18.
90. Dalton to Lushington, 30 September 1859, para 39.
91. Dalton, *Tribal History*, p. 184.

7

Conclusion

The period between 1821 and 1858 thus marks a glorious chapter in the history of Singhbhum when the inhabitants of this district whole-heartedly sought to withstand the in-roads of British imperialism. It asserted their political identity over a territory which they had carved out from the jungles with which it was originally clad and where they had evolved their distinct Ho identity, as different from their link with the Munda main stock. Songs appended with this work related their love for their own land as well as how they rallied to preserve its sanctity.

We learn that since their entry into Singhbhum they removed rocks, felled trees, drove away wild animals, made the land, habitable and settled their villages.[1] The people who had been uprooted and forced out of their earlier homes in the plateau naturally had the memory of the wrong done to them. This notion of wrong must have impinged into the corporate psyche of the people a sense of recoil and exclusiveness. This exclusiveness was reinforced by the geographical setting of their new land of habitat, protected by ranges of hills and thickness of forests, as if, the nature especially designing the area for them.[2] This land, as their folklore narrated, was encircled by ranges of hills, was full of rivers and streams carrying water, of clear breeze, of adequate rainfall and peace and plenty. This land was bounded by Anga Bira, Chari-Buru, and lofty Dalma and Singhasan hills and was watered by Baitarani, the river of Bongas, of Subarnarekha, Karo and Koel rivers.[3] This area, they believed, was named after the Singdar tree, with which the land was then abounded.[4] Around this land, their motherland, the Holy Ho land, their territorial identity fructified.[5]

Fed by the products of forests and tilling the fine open tract in most parts exceedingly productive[6] they lived an almost undisturbed life of 'peace and plenty'. They lived their own lives free and unrestrained, in the jungles or on hills and developed their personality marked by extraordinary strength, courage and endurance.[7] This land was naturally very dear to them. Through the strength of their arms they had occupied the area from Saraks, Gonds and Bhuiyans. With their traditional weapons of bow-arrow and battle-axe they had successfully foiled the efforts of Rajas of Chotanagpur, Mayurbhanj, Porahat and Seraikella to conquer this land. They had carried raids with impunity into the neighbourhood and earned the epithet of *Larka* Kols. This introduced a sense of confidence in their military prowess and faith in the capability of traditional weapons to fight the enemy. This confidence and faith were writ large on their valiant anti-British struggle profiled in the pages of this narrative.

The tribal culture and personality which grew over centuries stood threatened by the in-roads of more aggressive forces of expansion when the local chieftains joined the bandwagon of British imperialism during the second decade of the nineteenth century. The tribal resistance failed to halt the protégés of the mighty Imperium when the Agreement of 1821 imposed for the first time foreign rule on them. They were forced to pay taxes, a system which was unpalatable to them due to the lack of any such tradition in their polity. And later when the British manoeuvred to subjugate their land, the tribals naturally found their land and culture defiled and threatened. The initial failure to resist the local chiefs and then the British between 1821 and 1837 did not dampen their spirits. They united under the banner of Arjun Singh once again to protect their motherland.

The inhabitants of Singhbhum had primarily no central figure to organize this popular resistance. They had only their village and *pir* heads, and no authority beyond that as the symbol of unity and solidarity. The popular resistance was therefore organized around many local leaders and in many cases in spite of Mundas and Mankis. The unity and solidarity seemed to have been almost the spontaneous outcome of the inbuilt corporate and egalitarian tribal mechanism of life evolved over centuries. The basis of this ethos was the tribal communal life built around the three graded institutions of family, *Haga* and *Hatu*. Patriarchal family formed the base of this structure. Ownership of property was familial and not individual. A Ho was enjoined by custom to worship the family deity in the family *ading* and after death he was buried in the family *sasan*. He was then linked to the bigger unit of *Haga*. He was required to render all possible help during birth, marriage and funeral functions to its members. The extended family comprising his kinsmen residing in the same village called *killi* was the third bond to strengthen the ties of tribal solidarity up to the village level.[8] This bond was strengthened further by the observance of common socio-religious customs, festivals and particularly by communal hunting during the *chait parab*, when people departed to the hills north of Singhbhum for hunting.[9] The *pir* organization and tribal ethnic bonds over the areas where tribals predominated effected the inter-village and inter-*pir* solidarity which featured the popular resistance between 1821 and 1858. The circulation of battle arrow through the villages worked as an effective mechanism to rope in villages and people.[10] The messages during the struggle transmitted through the beating of drums must have been utilised to their advantage as done by the autochthones in Santal Pargana in 1855.[11] But this popular resistance was often distinguished by the transcendence of ethnic bonds. As related before not the Hos alone, but the Bhumijs, Santals and Gowallas participated in the fight against enemies in 1834. The apex was, however, the movement of 1857-58 when the Singhbhum struggle was organised under a central leadership and featured by tribal and non-tribal unity.

The uniqueness of the struggle, however, lay in the socialisation of the idea of wrong and willingness to fight. This was epitomised by the songs the local bards composed and men and women sang through the length and breadth to inspire the people. They knew that the *Telengas* were their enemies.

Due to them 'the whole land is ablaze, the whole kingdom is on fire'. They had forcibly entered their motherland and defiled her.[12] Sisters reminded that their hamlets were occupied and their sylvan freedom was about to be robbed by foreigners.[13] So the inhabitants of Singhbhum, the Munda brethren, were asked to wake up to the reality of wrong and the danger of impending bondage. They were asked to be united in resistance, to take up bow-arrow and battleaxes and fight the hated *Telengas* and to drive them away from their soil.[14] Sisters called their brothers to entrust the field and domestic work to their care so that they could be mentally and physically free to march ahead towards the battlefields and whole-heartedly fight the enemies to save their motherland, the Holy Ho land from the tentacles of the abominable foreigners.[15] Not this alone when the need arose women and children joined their male folk in their booths and retired into their jungle hide outs to fight for the preservation of their most prized freedom, nature's unique gift to them.

The archival materials invoked by this narrative when read along with their folklore underline the territorial sensitivity which played a crucial role not only in the Ho anti-British struggle narrated here but continued to remain central to the collective self of the Ho, rather of the indigenous in general.

NOTES AND REFERENCES

1. Appendix, Song III.
2. Bradley Birt, *Chota Nagpore: A Little known Province of the Empire*, p. 85.
3. Appendix, Song III.
4. *Ibid.*, Song-II. This adds a new element to the naming of Singhbhum, after *Sing Bonga* or the Singh dynasty or being the lion land. P.C. Roy Choudhury, *Bihar District Gazetteers, Singhbhum*, Patna, 1958, p. 2; O'Malley, *Bengal District Gazetteers*, p. 1; Hunter, *Imperial Gazetteer of India*, vol. XII, p. 529.
5. *Ibid.*, Songs I-III.
6. Lt. Tickell, 'Memoir on the Ho-desum (improperly called Kolehan)', *Journal of the Asiatic Society of Bengal*, vol. IX, pt. II, 1840. pp. 696-99.

7. Bradley Birt, *Chota Nagpore*, p. 85.
8. D.N. Majumdar, *The Affairs of a Tribe*, Lucknow, 1950, pp.105 and 286.
9. Tickell, 'Memoir', pp. 785-88.
10. R. Guha, *Elementary Aspects of Peasant Insurgency in Colonial India*, OUP, Delhi, 1983, pp. 53, 63.
11. *Ibid.*, p. 129.
12. Appendix, Song I.
13. *Ibid.*, Song II.
14. *Ibid.*, Song I.
15. *Ibid.*, Song II.

Appendix

Song I

Delayo Singh Disum Nodo Ko,
Delayo Birid Pe I.
Delayo Nabu Disum Munda Ko,
Delayo Payaren Pe II.

Sar Kapi Sabe Keh Te ga,
Delayo Birid Pe I.
Jonom Disum Lagid Te ga,
Delayo Payaren Pe II.

Disum Tabu Loh Tana ga,
Rayji Tabu Bale Tana I.
Nabu Disum Tala Te ga,
Telenga—Ko Bolo Tana II.

Telenga—Ko Har Gidi Ko Pe,
Jonom Disum Lagid—Te I.
Sar Kapi Sabeh Keh Te ga,
Telenga—Ko Hare Ko—Pe II

Awake, awake and beware O you inhabitants of Singhbhum
Those who are still asleep—awake
Awake and advance people of the Ho land and
You, brethren Mundas, awake.

Take up arms Take bows and arrows and battle-axes
Awake and be armed
For the dear Motherland be armed and bravely march
The whole land is ablaze, the whole kingdom is on fire

The whole land is ablaze, the whole kingdom is on fire
The Telengas have defiled the soil
They have entered the Ho land.
Turn, turn the alien away, far, far away

O brethren take up bows and arrows and battle-axes,
To drive the alien Telengas away,—Out
of our sacred land

Song II: Misi Ko Durang (Song of the sisters)

Note Hasa Ning-Ge Nele, Pieti Kami Ning-Ge Sabe
Juno Baring Senow-me Larai Tandi Te I
Disum do go Tane – Tana, Nutu Do Ko Nesere Tana
Jonom Disum Lagid – Ete Jugo Senow-me II
Kora Nonem Jonoma Kana
Jugo Bareng Senow-me Telenga Larai Te I
Sar Kapi Sabe Keh Te
Jugo Bareng Senow-me Telenga Larai Te II
Note Hasain Nele Geya, Paiti Kamin Sabe Geya
Jugo Bareng Senow-me Disum Larai Te I

The Sisters' Song

Leave the work of the fields and the gardens;
Entrust us with these duties domestic —
And you, brethren, haste and march to the
battlefield
Aliens are intruding upon our Motherland;
Foreigners are occupying our hamlets;
To save the land rush on, march onwards,
Born as males you must fight for Freedom.
March on, brothers on to fight the Telengas
So take bows and arrows and take the
Battle-axe.
March on undaunted and meet the
Telengas in battle.
Be sure, be confident, that we shall mind

All that has to be done in the fields and
at home;
Be sure and haste, Ye brothers march on—
To quell the foe—for the dear Motherland,
The cherished Ho-land.

Song III: Niral Disum (The Holy Land)

Sing-Suba-re Sing-Bonga Seba Ka-te Disum Keda
Sing Disum Nutum Te Ko Nutum-E-Tada I
Bir-buru Tandi Ka-te Kula Buru Har Ka-te
Bir-Ko Tala-mala Re Ko Disum-E-Keda II

Diri Daru Aming Ka-te, Gora Loyong Tandi Ko Re
Bera Nari Ko Bari Leda Disum Tala Re I
Bir-buru te Biura-kan, Gara Nari-te Singara Kan
Nimin Bugin Disum-e-Tain Disum Baiya Kan II

Hoyo Gama Bugin Geya, Joma Nuiya Lali Geya
Nimin Bugin Disum-e-ren Jonoma Kana I
Anga-Bira Chari-Buru, Dalma-chutina Sings-so-te
Bakai Biura Kan II

Sona Gara Samom-rakha, Bonga-ko-Gara Baitoroni
Karo-Kuili Marang-Gara-te Sajao Singara Kan. I

The Holy Land

Under the great tree we prayed and prayed to *Sing/Bonga*
And shaped the Motherland with His blessings,
and after the "Sing" tree the land was named Sing-bhoom.
Many a rock had to be removed and many forests felled,
Tigers, bears and wild animals had to be driven away—
To make the land in the hills and dales habitable.
So was the Holy-Ho-Land carved out of the
dales and dense forests.
And through incessant and unceasing labour
The uplands, slopes and glades were cleared of
stones and jungles

and took the shape of low or sloping fields;
So fresh and full of verdure and autumn's rich harvest
Encircled with ranges of hills and in the
midst of sylvan solitude
where rivers and streams flow with crystal clearness,
This beautiful, this Holy land has been
converted into our abode.
Bracing is the breeze here and sufficient is the rain,
Peace and plenty have dwelt here in;
And fortunate are we to be born in this beautiful land
Anga-Bira, Chari-Buru and the lofty Dalma
and Singhasan hills;
The gleaming golden river Subarnarekha
and Baitarani, the river of *Bongas*
Karo, Koel and many a meandering stream
Flow through and adorn this beautiful land of ours,
This wonderful, this holy-Ho-land, the land of our birth

Glossary

Adibasi	Autochthonous people, designated as the Scheduled Tribe
Ading	Portion of the house preserved for the ancestral spirits
Barkandaze	A matchlock man, commonly applied to a native of India
Bonga	Spirit
Challan	Despatch
Dafadar	Commandant of a body of horse, a police officer
Dak	Post, post office
Dhan	Paddy
Diku	Outsider, more often a non-Adibasi
Dobhasias	Interpreters
Garh	A fort, mud fort
Ghat	Mountain pass
Gowala	Cowherd
Haga	Agnate
Hatu	Village
Ilaka	Subdivision comprising a group of villages under a Manki
Kabuliyat	A written agreement
Khass	The lands held and cultivated themselves by zamindars
Khundi	Weight equivalent to 20 seers
Khuntkatti	Original clearance
Killedar	Commandant or holder of a fort
Killi	Clan or sept among the Hos, Adibasis
Larka	Fighting
Lakhiraj	A revenue-free grant
Malguzari	Rent

Manki	Head of *pir*
Munda	Head of a village
Nala	An artificial channel or a small rivulet, commission of rent
Pargana	Area comprising many villages, a *pir*
Parwana	Summons, warrant
Patta	A deed of lease
Pir	A cluster of villages resembling a pargana
Sanad	A grant
Sarbaraharkar	A manager, a steward
Sardar	Chief, Leader of men
Sasan	A burial ground of Hos
Sing-Bonga	Sun god
Subedar	A native officer in the Company's army, holding a rank equivalent to a captain
Tal	Palm

Bibliography

PRIMARY SOURCES

Government Records—Manuscripts and Printed Reports

Bihar State Archives, Patna

Manuscripts

South West Frontier Political Despatch Register
Vol. 25 from 12 August 1817 to 15 December 1818
Vol. 26 from 6 October 1819 to 10 November 1820
Vol. 27 from 20 April 1820 to 7 June 1821
Vol. 28 from 10 May 1820 to 5 April 1821
Vol. 29 from 2 April 1821 to 10 December 1821
Vol. 125 from 2 May 1833 to 16 April 1835
Vol. 126 from 11 May 1836 to 23 September 1840
Vol. 127 from 7 January 1837 to 28 September 1839
Vol. 145 from 24 December 1831 to 21 May 1833
Vol. 231 from 13 May 1837 to 1 December 1840

Printed Source

Spare Copies of Porahat Papers from 1857-62

West Bengal State Archives, Calcutta

Bengal Judicial General letters to the Court of Directors from 3 January to 31 December 1832, Vol. 14 Letter Nos. 19, 23, Judicial Department

Bengal Judicial General letters to the Court of Directors from 17 March 1835 to 18 November 1836, Vol. 17, Letter No. 14, Judicial Department

Reports/Gazetteers/Memorial

Craven, J.A. *Final Report on the Settlement of the Kolhan Government Estate* 1897, Calcutta, 1898.

Hunter, W.W. *The Imperial Gazetteer of India*, Vol. XII, London, 1887.

Hunter, W.W. *A Statistical Account of Bengal*, Vol. XVII, Concept Publishing Company, Delhi, 1976.

McPherson, T.S. *Final Report on the operations for the preparation of a record of rights in Pargana Porahat, district of Singhbhum 1905-7*, Calcutta, 1906.

Maharaja of Mayurbhanj, *Secret Memorial of the Mayurbhanj State to H.E. The Rear Admiral the Right Honourable Viscount Mountbatten of Burma, Viceroy and Governor-General of India and Crown Representative*, Baripada, Mayurbhanj State, 29 July 1947.

O'Malley, L.S.S. *Bengal District Gazetteers Singhbhum, Seraikela and Kharsawan*, The Bengal Secretariat Book Depot, Calcutta, 1910.

Prasad, C.B. *Final Report on Survey and Settlement Operations in the District of Singhbhum 1958-1965*, Secretariat Press, Patna, 1970.

Reid, J. *Final Report on the Survey and Settlement Operations in the District of Ranchi 1902-1910*, Bengal Secretariat Book Depot, Calcutta, 1912.

Ricketts, H. (ed.), *Report on the district of Singhbhum. Selection from the Records of the Bengal Government*, No. XVI, Calcutta, 1854.

Roy Choudhury, P.C. Bihar District Gazetteers Singhbhum, Superintendent Secretariat Press, Patna, 1958.

Roy Choudhury, P.C. *Singhbhum Old Records*, Patna, 1958.

Taylor, J.H. *Final Report on the Survey and Settlement Operations in the Porahat Estate, District Singhbhum 1900-1903*, Calcutta, 1904.

Tuckey, A.D. *Final Report on the Resettlement of the Kolhan Government Estate in the District of Singhbhum 1913-1918*, Superintendent, Government Printing, Bihar and Orissa, Patna, 1920.

SECONDARY SOURCES

Published

Aitchison, C.U. *A Collection of Treatises, Engagements and Sanads relating to India and Neighbouring Countries*, Vol. II, Government of India, Central Publication Branch, Calcutta, 1930.

Bhadra, G. 'Four Rebels of Eighteen-Fifty Seven', in *Subaltern Studies IV*, Oxford University Press (OUP), Delhi, 1990.

Bradley-Birt, F.B. *Chota Nagpore A Little Known Province of the Empire*, London, 1903.

Buchanan, F. *Journal of Patna and Gaya in 1811-12*, Superintendent, Government Printing, Bihar and Orissa, Patna, 1925.

Buckland, C.E. *Bengal under the Lieutenant-Governors from 1854-1898*, Vols. 1-2, Calcutta, 1902.

Dalton, E.T. *Descriptive Ethnology of Bengal*, Calcutta, 1872 and also *Tribal History of Eastern India (original title Descriptive Ethnology of Bengal)*, Cosmo Publication, Delhi, 1973.

Datta, K.K. *Unrest Against British Rule in Bihar 1831-1859*, Patna, 1957.

Datta, K.K. *Anti-British Plots and Movements before 1857*, Meerut, 1970.

Fuchs, S. *Rebellious Prophets: A Study of Messianic Movements in Indian Religions*, Asia Publishing House, 1965.

Guha, R. *Elementary Aspects of Peasant Insurgency in Colonial India*, OUP, Delhi, 1983.

Jha, J.C. *Kol Insurrection in Chotanagpur*, Calcutta, 1964.

Jha, J.C. *The Tribal Revolt of Chotanagpur (1831-32)*, K.P. Jayaswal Research Institute, Patna, 1987.

Majumdar, D.N. *A Tribe in Transition: Study in Cultural Pattern*, Longmans Green and Co. Ltd., Calcutta, 1937.

Majumdar, D.N. *The Affairs of a Tribe*, Calcutta, 1950.

Majumdar, R.C. *The Sepoy Mutiny and the Revolt of 1857*, Calcutta, 1957.

Majumdar, R.C. *History of the Freedom Movement in India*, Vol. I, Firma K.L. Mukhopadhyay, Calcutta, 1962.

Malleson, G.B. *History of the Indian Mutiny*, 3 Vols.

Risley, H.H. *The Tribes and Castes of Bengal*, Vol. I, Calcutta, 1981.

Roy, S.C. *The Mundas and their Country*, Calcutta, 1912 and also Asia Publishing House, Calcutta, 1970.

Roy, S.C. *Oraon Religion and Customs*, Edition Indian, Calcutta, 1972.

Roy Choudhury, P.C. *1857 in Bihar (Chotanagpur and Santhal Parganas)*, Patna, 1959.

Sahu, M. *The Kolhan under the British Rule*, Calcutta, 1985.

Sen, S.N. *Eighteen Fifty-seven*, Government of India, 1957.

Singh, C.P. *The Ho Tribe of Singhbhum*, Classical Publications, New Delhi, 1978.

Singh, K.S. 'State-Formation in Tribal Society: Some Preliminary Observations', *Journal of Indian Anthropological Society*, Vol. 6, 1971.

Singh, K.S. 'The Munda Land System and Revenue Reforms in Chotanagpur during 1869-1908' *vide* R.S. Sharma (ed.), *Land Revenue in India: Historical Studies*, Motilal Banarsidass, Patna, 1971.

Singh Deo, B. *The Vulture-Lamb Policy and The Lost State of Porahat-Singhbhum or Porahat and Her Remains*, Calcutta, 1930.

Singhdeo, T.N.N. *Singhbhum, Seraikela and Kharsawan—Through the Ages*, Calcutta, No date.

Sinha, S. 'State Formation and Rajput Myth in Tribal Central India', *Man in India*, Vol. 42, No. I, March, 1962.

Sinha, S. 'Tribe, Caste and Peasant Continua', *Man in India*, Vol. 45, No. I, March 1965.

Sinha, S.C., Sen, J. and Panchabhai, S. 'The Concept of Diku among the Tribes of Chotanagpur', *Man in India*, Vol. 49, No. 2, April-June 1969.

Sur, N. 'Chotanagpur and the Rising of 1857', *Bengal Past and Present*, January-December 1986.

Tickell, Lt. S.R. 'Memoir on the Ho Desum' (improperly called Kolehan)', *Journal of Asiatic Society of Bengal*, Vol. XI, Part II, (1840).

Wilson, H.H. *A Glossary of Judicial and Revenue Terms of British India*, Calcutta, 1940.

Index